ONLY WINGS

BOLD AND UNUSUAL RECIPES

A COOKBOOK
by QUENTIN ERICKSON

ONLY WINGS: BOLD AND UNUSUAL RECIPES

Published by Entrée Press, LLC.

ONLY WINGS: BOLD AND UNUSUAL RECIPES

ISBN 978-0-9773344-1-4

Printed in the United States of America

*For my wonderful wife, Mary, and my sons, Rene and Alex,
who have joined me over the course of many years,
enthusiastically, on this culinary journey.*

*And a sincere thank you to Doug Schenkelberg,
my all-weather friend, who, for this project, provided consultation
and sound advice on various aspects of cooking and recipes.*

QUENTIN ERICKSON, is a globe-trotting, life-long foodie and improvisational cook who is bringing his mantra *"Variety in food is the spice of life!"* to all who love culinary adventure. His exploratory cookbooks focus on the myriad of options and wealth of inspiration available to us all.

Entrée Press Online

Visit www.EntreePress.com to explore additional "Play with your food!" interactive cookbooks.

CONTENTS

THE FIRST BITE

BEVERAGE WINGS

FRUIT WINGS

VEGETABLE AND NUT WINGS

HONEY WINGS

WING DIPPING SAUCES

APPENDIX 145

THE FIRST BITE

"Cooking is like love. It should be entered into with abandon or not at all."
Harriet Van Horne

"I feel a recipe is only a theme, which an intelligent cook can play each time with a variation."
Madame Benoit

These two quotes eloquently encapsulate my personal philosophy on cooking and the intent of this cookbook. Cooking, like life, is a great adventure that should be undertaken with great gusto.

My hobby over the years has been collecting and cooking recipes, with a focus on the unusual, the outlandish and the novel. Early on, I found that I derived more satisfaction from experimentation than with following the "paint-by-numbers" method.

Substituting ingredients, altering ingredient amounts, changing cooking methods—it has all become a happy obsession. Some basic kitchen and grilling equipment, a well-stocked pantry and a vivid imagination can result in stellar cuisine.

As a result of this on-going experimentation, I have become a better cook, I have a lot more fun in the kitchen, and my palate has become much more refined. I believe that you too can achieve these same benefits by embracing an adventurous attitude. These recipes should be seen as the jumping-off point of *your* great adventure.

Explore, experiment, be bold and find inspiration in the subtle and the obvious. Cooking, as is life, is a journey whose path can be both sweet and savory and whose destination is satisfaction. When you pour your heart and soul into cooking, the rewards are immense.

USING THE COOKBOOK

As I experiment with my recipes, I do a pretty fair job of documenting substitutions and other alterations I've made, although sometimes the scribbles can be a bit indecipherable. The page formatting of the recipes in this collection is intended to directly assist you on your journey of exploration. Use these pages to shop for ingredients, capture the thoughts of dinner guests, document cooking dates, and most importantly, record your experimentation for future reference.

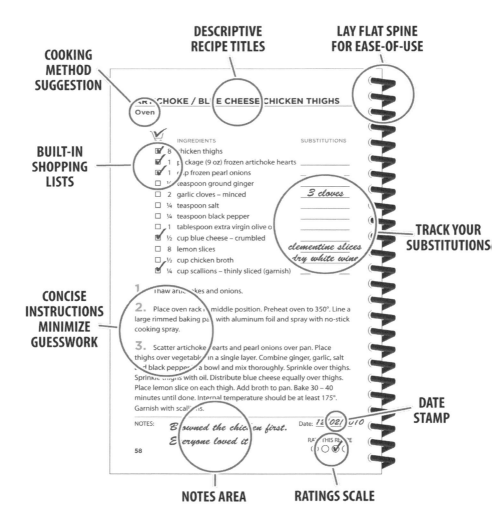

DESCRIPTIVE RECIPE TITLES

LAY FLAT SPINE FOR EASE-OF-USE

COOKING METHOD SUGGESTION

BUILT-IN SHOPPING LISTS

TRACK YOUR SUBSTITUTIONS

CONCISE INSTRUCTIONS MINIMIZE GUESSWORK

DATE STAMP

NOTES AREA

RATINGS SCALE

PLAY WITH YOUR FOOD

The ingredient, flavoring and cooking process combinations available to you are virtually infinite, bounded only by the ingredients you happen to have on hand. Take advantage of that variety. Recipes are but a framework to build upon and to deviate from, to alter and to modify to your own tastes and satisfaction.

Make adjustments and refinements to the recipe until the dish is perfect for you. It is a dash to the cupboard for spices, to the refrigerator for new ingredients or to the wine rack for a splash of wine. Experiment, enjoy, fail and then prevail. Innovate, experiment, compare recipes, combine recipes, feed the failures to the dog and the successes to royalty (your in-laws). Be bold. Do. Try. Win!

SUBSTITUTION REVOLUTION

Your primary method for creating culinary creations unique to you and your tastes is through ingredient substitution. Substitutions can have a subtle or profound impact on the flavor profile, texture, healthiness and even the cooking time of recipes. By fully embracing experimentation and improvisation, you will have more fun in the kitchen while becoming a better cook, you'll develop a more sophisticated palate, and you'll create a collection of recipes that are uniquely yours.

There are other reasons you might want to substitute an ingredient (other than for the sheer enjoyment of tasting your successful creations). You may have health concerns, you may be missing an ingredient, or you may not like a particular taste.

In the appendix, you'll find a wealth of information that will get you going in the right direction. The material is not exhaustive, nor is it meant to be. It represents only a small portion of the options available to you, but it will be a solid reference for you in your adventures. Use your imagination, improvise, explore!

PLAYING DRESS-UP

Diners eat first with their eyes. If your food looks unappetizing, you've gotten off on the wrong taste bud. The way your meal is presented affects the way the diners think the food will taste.

The Plan

Preplan the presentation of the dish from the time you begin its preparation. Have a visualization of the completed meal in mind. If you are serving hot food, plating has to be done quickly. Consider building a "practice plate" before plating all the meals.

The Plate

Use a plate large enough to allow you to use "white space" as a design element. You don't want to crowd the food. Allow the food to "breathe" on the plate. Plates that are white or neural in color will allow the food to stand front and center. The shape of the plate should be simple as well. The focus should always be on the food.

Consider heating the plates in an electric oven if that particular food combination can benefit from a warm plate that keeps the components warm during serving and on into the meal. Preheat the oven to 150° and warm the plates for 5 minutes or so. Be extra careful handling the hot plates.

Pay attention to how the plate will be oriented when served. Use the front of the plate to highlight the main focus of the meal. If you are going to add height to the food, placing the height at the back of the plate will add to the appeal.

Plating

First and foremost, keep it simple. Unless you have a kitchen staff, you are going to want to be able to plate quickly, while the food is still hot. Start from the middle of the plate and work your way outward. Don't fuss too much with the plated food, you'll only make things worse.

COLOR: Select foods that add visual interest through color. Poultry and fish can have fairly bland colors. Colorful vegetables, peppers and fruit wedges can add that splash of color the plate is calling for.

SHAPE: Take the shape of the foods into consideration. Round meatballs, round Brussels sprouts and round potatoes on a plate do not an exciting plate make. Take a few moments to cut and shape the food into different figures and sizes to create visual appeal.

SYMMETRY: The house says odd always beats even: five meatballs are more pleasing to the eye than four; three colors on a plate are more interesting than two. Apply this maxim to any plating variable.

TEXTURE: Though not a visual presentation element, don't neglect texture. A well balanced plate requires variety in texture. Puréed squash, baked salmon and whipped potatoes may taste great together but will not provide any variety in mouth feel.

SAUCES: Go easy on the sauce, as too much sauce on the plate may give the impression that you are trying to hide a poorly prepared meal. Sauces are generally placed underneath the meat. If you lean the meat against the starch element of the meal, you'll keep the meat from becoming too saturated in the sauce, and the diner will better be able to view its preparation.

NEATNESS: And finally, take the time to be sure your plates are neat and free of drips and spills. No slopped sauces or stray pieces—your finished plate should be a work of art, with you the acclaimed artist.

Garnishes

Garnishes provide a great opportunity for adding that dash of panache. A quick shave of parmesan cheese, a sprig of parsley or cilantro, a wedge of avocado, a dollop of sour cream, a dash of paprika—all just a taste of the available garnishes. Garnishes are just the right touch of color, texture and flavor. All garnishes should be of the edible variety—avoid items like rosemary sprigs or flower pedals, for instance.

Inspiration

As always, inspiration is where you find it. Look to food magazines for ideas on arranging food on the plate, pay attention to the plating techniques at your favorite restaurant, and experiment with your own plates. You are only limited by attentiveness and imagination.

TO GRILL OR NOT TO GRILL

Chicken wing tartare is not an option. We know that chicken has to be cooked somehow. This cookbook provides suggested cooking methods for each recipe. These are only suggestions! Altering cooking methods is another opportunity for experimentation. These chicken wing recipes are generally interchangeable between oven, grill, slow cooker and deep frying.

When cooking wings in the oven, a relatively steady, even, medium temperature produces the best result. Wings should not be cooked too quickly or too slowly. If cooked too quickly, they can become tough and dry. If cooked too slowly, the wing meat and skin can turn mushy.

If you plan on translating oven, grill or slow cooker recipes to the deep fryer, do not apply any ingredients to the wings prior to immersion in hot oil. Wings to be deep fried should be clean and dry. Combine the other recipe ingredients into a sauce and toss wings to coat after deep frying.

If you plan on translating grill, oven or deep fry recipes to the slow cooker, here are suggested recipe modifications:

- Reduce liquids by about 25 percent. There is very little evaporation in slow cooking.

- Reduce by approximately one half the recommended quantity of whole leaves and spices. Add additional herbs and spices in the last hour of cooking for a flavor boost.

Whatever cooking method you choose, the internal temperature of wings should be at least 165°, and the juices should run clear. Use a meat thermometer to ensure doneness.

TIME OUT

Different situations can influence cooking times. For example, not all ovens are accurate—they can vary by many degrees plus or minus the set temperature. You will need to learn the idiosyncrasies of your particular oven.

Foods cook more slowly at higher altitudes, so depending on the nature of your oven and your altitude, cooking times could vary by as much as 20%.

If you use a convection oven, cooking times will definitely be different from those of a conventional oven. Refer to the manufacturers' recommendations about cooking times.

Cooking times for bone-in meats is longer as the bone absorbs a lot of heat and does not conduct heat effectively.

Meat that has been brined will cook more quickly. There is speculation that the extra moisture in the tissue, with its high heat conductivity qualities, accelerates the cooking process.

Other factors that influence cooking time include the thickness of the cut, temperature of the meat when you begin cooking, how many times you open the cooking equipment to take a peek, the quantity of other foods being cooked at the same time, and the fat content of the item being cooked.

A meat thermometer is now standard equipment in every kitchen. If you don't have one, pick one up the next time you leave the house! Using a meat thermometer is quite straight forward: place the probe in the thickest part of the cut and away from bone. See Table 5 in the Appendix for recommended safe internal temperatures for cooked meats.

FINDING YOUR STYLE

Perhaps the most enjoyable aspect of constant exploration and improvisation, other than the well-deserved accolades of dinner guests, is that through exploration you will be developing your own voice, your own brand of confidence, your own style.

"Style" in cooking has many faces. Do you prefer the comfort provided by comfort food and a satisfied brood? Do you concentrate on healthy fare and fresh produce? Does your idea of cooking involve stoking coals and managing the temperature of a grill, regardless of mother nature's plans?

Do you prefer quick and easy meals, your pantry overflowing with instant potatoes, instant rice and instant gratification? Do you prefer cooking everything from scratch, time at the market and in the kitchen be damned? Are you a study in culinary improvisation, working without a net, your pantry stocked with imported spices and exotic concoctions?

Do you define your style by an American regional cuisine? Cajun? New England? Southwestern? Or perhaps you prefer cooking with an international flair. French? Italian? Mexican? Szechuan?

Your individual cooking style will have elements of all of these definitions, and will continue to refine itself over time. As you develop your "style," be sure to place an emphasis on expanding your horizons. By bringing in influences from many sources, you'll develop a sense of the compatibility of different tastes, you will learn to intuitively develop your own recipes, and in the process, you will find more joy in the kitchen.

YOU HAVE GOOD TASTE

You have good taste. That much is obvious—you're reading this cookbook! Developing your culinary palate will (and should) be a life-long endeavor, and you should consider it one of the most gratifying journeys you will embark upon in life. I consider the ongoing development of my palate to be one of my life's great journeys.

Developing your palate is not as difficult as you might think. And it is not necessarily just about trying new foods. You can start by trying different varieties of foods you already enjoy. There are literally hundreds of varieties of cheeses, and multiple varieties of many basic vegetables. Go with what you know.

But eventually you will need to venture into the unknown. Give new and novel (to you) food the benefit of the doubt, and admit that someone, somewhere, must believe a particular item to be at least edible or it probably wouldn't be considered "food."

You may find delicious treats that you never knew existed, and you may find some food items that for you will be an acquired taste. Acquire that taste. A great pleasure of mine is turning palate-shy people into Brussels sprout eaters. Boiled until tender (the sprouts, not the people), sliced open and stuffed with blue cheese, crumbled bacon, and a grain or two of sea salt, then drizzled with olive oil and broiled until the cheese is bubbling—avowed sprouts haters will be lining up for the recipe!

Stop smoking, brush your tongue.

And finally, the more information you have, the better equipped you are to explore the culinary landscape. Seminars, foodie magazines, television shows, restaurants—inspiration is where you find it. Explore. Climb. Conquer!

1-2-3 TRINITY

A "trinity" is the combination of three essential ingredients as the flavoring base in a recipe, often created by sautéing a combination of any three aromatic vegetables, condiments, seasonings, herbs, or spices. Trinities are most typically used when creating sauces, soups, stew, and stir-fries.

Geographic regions often have a trinity of ingredients that comprise the flavor base of dishes for that cuisine. For example, if the recipe calls for a base of onion, bell pepper and celery it is a good bet it is a Louisiana Creole dish. This particular trinity combination is known as the "Holy Trinity." Create your own regional dishes by experimenting with "trinity" combinations of ingredients. See Table 6 in the Appendix for a list of trinity flavor bases from various cultures.

COOKING WITH HEAT

To regulate the heat in a recipe, increase or decrease any of the heat ingredients listed here. With the exception of horseradish and wasabi, they are chili pepper-based.

- Hot pepper sauce is a primary heat source in many recipes. It is basically chili peppers combined with tomatoes, onions, vinegar, sugar and spices.

- Cayenne pepper is a powder derived from several different chilies to produce a hot, fiery taste.

- Red pepper flakes are available as whole flakes, ground red pepper flakes or crushed red pepper flakes.

- Harissa sauce is a product from north Africa. It is flavorful and hot. It is made up of hot chili peppers, cumin, coriander, garlic, caraway and oil.

- Sriracha is the name of a hot sauce with a southeast Asian influence. It is a hot chili sauce made from dried chilies ground into a paste with garlic, vinegar, salt, sugar and other ingredients.

- Horseradish, commercially prepared, is recommended in this cookbook because it is handy and convenient. For a real jolt, though, try freshly-grated horseradish root.
- Wasabi, horseradish's Japanese cousin, will give a good jolt, too.

The heat of peppers can be softened by removing the seeds and ribs from the inside, but the flesh will still be hot. In general, the smaller the pepper and the narrower the shoulder near the stem, the hotter the bite, but some varieties will break the rules with a fiery surprise.

When working with fiery peppers, it's important to protect yourself by using eye protection and wearing latex or rubber gloves. After handling peppers, wash your hands carefully with plenty of soap and warm water before touching your eyes and mouth.

In the event the heat surpasses your tolerance level, a cold glass of milk—not water—can have a mitigating effect on the condition. Milk contains the protein casein which pulls the capsaicin (the active heat component of chili peppers) away from the burning taste buds. See Table 7 in the Appendix for a list of capsaicin levels in different peppers.

RUBS AND MARINADES AND BRINES, OH MY!

Rubs

Spice rubs can add a great deal of flavor to meat or fish dishes. The spices are generally course ground, and the mixture can also include various herbs, salt and crushed garlic. Adding sugar will cause the rub to caramelize during cooking. Adding oil will create a paste, which can help the rub adhere to the meat. Rubs are readily available at the supermarket, but creating your own is much more rewarding. Rubs can be sweet, spicy and everything in between. If you are adventurous, rubs on vegetables can be delicious.

Generally, the rub should not be applied any sooner than two hours before cooking, although some recipes recommend longer times. The rationale for applying the rub just before cooking is to eliminate the chance of the rub inducing texture changes in the meat.

I've found that brushing the food item with spicy mustard just prior to applying the rub not only helps the rub stick but also adds complexity of flavor.

Place the food item on a cooking rack and lay newspaper under the rack. The rub should be applied generously. What sticks on, sticks on, and what falls off, falls off. I have found that using a pizza red pepper flake shaker works great for dispensing the rub. Gently massaging the rub onto the surface will increase the amount of rub that adheres. Apply the rub to the top, bottom and edges of the food item. Minimize handling—the more you fuss, the more the rub will fall off. Reapply the spices that dropped onto the newspaper to minimize waste.

Marinades

Marinating is the process of flavoring food by soaking in heavily seasoned liquid before cooking. A marinade can be acidic if based on liquids such as vinegar or lemon juice, or enzymatic if made with ingredients such as papaya or pineapple.

The maximum marinating time for poultry, under any circumstances, is 3 hours. Any longer than 3 hours and the meat will become mushy. I recommend 8 hours marinating for ribs. Marinade can be used to tenderize tough cuts of meats, but marinate times are quite long when trying to tenderize (up to 24 hours), so is recommended for only the toughest cuts.

Flavors can be enhanced with sweeteners such as sugar, honey and syrups. Soy sauce is a fantastic marinade ingredient. Herbs and spices commonly used in marinating are oil-soluble and their flavor is released when mixed with oil.

When marinating, use a large re-sealable plastic bag to hold the marinade and meat. Before placing the bag in the refrigerator, set the bag on a plate to avoid a mess in the event of a bag leak. If the meat cuts are too large for the bag, cut the meat to fit. If jumbo bags are not available, any container will work if it can be sealed tightly.

Brines

Like marinating, brining is a process in which poultry, pork or seafood is soaked in a liquid solution before cooking. Meats with high fat content like beef, lamb and duck, tend not to benefit from brining. The basic brine is salt, sugar and water. I prefer sea salt and brown sugar, as they impart more flavor. Combine the ingredients in a ratio of 1 cup salt, 1 cup sugar to 2 quarts water.

Determine how much brine you'll need to completely submerge the food item in your selected, sealable container. Mix the salt, sugar and water (plus any other spices) together, heat the mixture to dissolve the salt and sugar, and let cool completely. Combine the brine and food in the container, and then place a ceramic plate or bowl on the food to submerge it, and place in the fridge. For large items like a whole turkey, use a cooler, adding ice to the cooler to keep it chilled for 8 to 12 hours. For small birds or poultry portions, brine for around 3 hours, and for pork chops or tenderloins, brine for around 6 hours.

The salt in the brine works to hydrate the cells of the muscle tissue by drawing water into the tissues through osmosis, and also denatures the cell proteins, further helping the meat to retain moisture during cooking.

Regardless of the science involved, it works! If you've never brined a turkey, you've missed a moist, mystical experience. Because a brine opens up the meat to hydration, if you add other herbs and spices to the brine, these additional flavor additives with also deeply infuse into the meat.

INSPIRATION IS WHERE YOU FIND IT

I traveled the globe during my hitch in the Navy, and I traveled the width and breadth of the United States in my decades-long civilian career. I have been privileged to experience a bounty of diverse foods and cultures, and to share those experiences with many friends, customers and employees.

Some "not-to-be-forgotten" culinary experiences include:

- A black bean soup in Indianapolis, Indiana
- Crawfish in restaurants along Lake Pontchartrain, Louisiana
- Baby back ribs in San Antonio, Texas
- A turtle soup in St. Louis, Missouri
- A steak flambé in a second-story restaurant overlooking the Ramblas in Barcelona, Spain
- Oysters in a bar in Athens, Greece
- Abalone on the wharf in San Francisco, California
- A crème brûlée at the Ritz-Carlton in Chicago, Illinois
- A gumbo in Greenfield, North Carolina
- A hearts of palm salad at the Breakers Hotel in West Palm Beach, Florida
- A rack of lamb in Neenah, Wisconsin

  . . . and the list goes on

I ate fine and not-so-fine food as I dined at a myriad of restaurants and resorts. These experiences all had an impact on my personal cooking style. Always, I would try to choose a menu item that would give me a new experience. These unique dishes provided ideas and inspiration. Inspiration is where you find it. Use the skills of others to your own advantage.

WRESTLING RECIPES

LOOK BEFORE YOU LEAP

A highly recommended practice is to scan and survey a recipe before cooking it. You don't want to find midway though cooking that you are missing a key ingredient or that you are about to add an ingredient you don't like! Gather your ingredients and plan your substitutions.

A PLACE FOR EVERYTHING

The French term "mise en place" literally means "putting in place." For us it means organizing and arranging all ingredients for a recipe, prior to cooking, and placing them in the food preparation area in the order listed in the recipe. I also pre-measure all the ingredients and place them in small bowls or cups to use in sequence as I prepare a recipe.

ANYONE CAN ADD, BUT CAN YOU SUBTRACT?

It is simple to revise the profile of a recipe by adding or adjusting ingredients. Once all the ingredients are mixed, however, it is very difficult to eliminate or mask a flavor. Exercise a bit of caution when substituting ingredients — add a bit at a time and taste as you go.

WINGING IT

WHEN WINGS TOOK OFF

Although fried chicken, including wings, has long been a staple of southern cooking, the first serving of Buffalo wings is frequently attributed to the Anchor Bar in Buffalo, New York, in late 1964.

Wings are the most popular appetizer in restaurants across the nation. One nation restaurant franchise is dedicated (almost) solely to chicken wings, and virtually every Chinese buffet serves wings. The National Chicken Council estimates that on Super Bowl Sunday 2010, Americans polished off over 100 million pounds of chicken wings—about 1.25 billion wing portions!

My interest in chicken wings began in 1963 when a friend insisted that wings are the best part of the chicken. The current popularity of chicken wings would imply that he was probably correct! Since that fateful conversation in 1963, I have collected chicken wing recipes with a passion.

There seems to be no end to the flavor profiles that one can impart to this humble little appendage. I have satiated the hunger of many willing wing eaters at numerous events, picnics and family gatherings. You will, too.

SAFETY FIRST

- Uncooked, thawed wings can be refrigerated for a maximum of two days.

- Frozen uncooked wings should be used within two or three months. Frozen cooked wings should be used within a month.

- Use a meat thermometer to obtain precise temperatures. The cooking times recommended in recipes are approximations. Wings are ready when meat is no longer pink, juices run clear and internal temperature is at least 165°.

- Wrapping wings in foil after cooking will help retain heat. The internal temperature will continue to increase as wings rest.

- Once cooked, wings should be kept either hot or promptly refrigerated or frozen. Cooked wings can be refrigerated for up to 2 days.

- Reheat wings in a covered baking dish in a 375° oven or in a microwave set on high until meat internal temperature is 165°.

PROPER PREP

- All recipes in this collection are designed to serve 4 people.

- Wash hands before and after handling chicken wings.

- Twelve medium size wings weigh about two pounds. After cutting, the twenty-four wing segments will fit comfortably on a baking pan or in a large skillet.

- Rinse wings to remove extraneous material and pat dry with paper towels. Thoroughly dry the wings to achieve proper browning. Rinsing does not kill bacteria—cooking to 165° kills bacteria.

- Use a jumbo re-sealable plastic bag or a 1-gallon re-sealable plastic bag when marinating wings. Squeeze out excess air before sealing bag.

See Table 8 in the Appendix for a list of recommended kitchen and grill equipment.

KEEPIN' IT CRISPY

Because deep frying wings in the home, in addition to being a messy process, has a high probability for burn injuries, the majority of the cooking processes in this collection reference other cooking methods like baking and grilling. You can still achieve crispy wings without deep frying by utilizing your broiler or grill. Once the wings are cooked, broil wings 2 or 3 minutes on each side in the oven, or finish off the wings with 5 or 6 minutes on the grill.

WING DIPS

Be sure to take a look at the blue cheese and other dips at the end of the Recipes section. These are dip variations I have enjoyed over years and all are delicious. Tip: I purchase block blue cheese and crumble it myself, as pre-crumbled blue cheese is considerably more expensive.

Enjoy!

BEVERAGE
WINGS

APPLE JUICE / SALSA WINGS

Slow Cooker

INGREDIENTS			SUBSTITUTIONS
☐	12	wings segmented, tips discarded – rinsed/dried	
☐	¾	cup apple juice	_____
☐	1	jar (16 ounce) salsa – medium	_____
☐	¼	cup Dijon mustard	_____
☐	½	cup brown sugar – packed	_____
☐	1	teaspoon onion power	_____
☐	½	teaspoon garlic powder	_____
☐	1	teaspoon Worcestershire sauce	_____

1. Combine all ingredients except wings in a slow cooker and blend thoroughly. Taste, adjust flavoring.

2. Add wings to slow cooker. Cook on low 3 – 5 hours until wings are done. Turn wings midway through cooking. Internal temperature of wings should be at least 165°. Resist removing lid too often. Slow cooking requires internal heat and condensation.

3. Remove wings with a slotted spoon. Platter wings and cover with aluminum foil until ready to serve.

NOTES:

Date: _____

RATE THIS RECIPE
○ ○ ○ ○ ○

BEER / YOGURT / HOT SAUCE WINGS
Marinate I Oven

		INGREDIENTS	SUBSTITUTIONS
☐	12	wings segmented, tips discarded – rinsed/dried	
☐	1	bottle (12 ounce) beer	_____
☐	4	tablespoons hot pepper sauce – divided	_____
☐	1	teaspoon salt	_____
☐	1	teaspoon black pepper	_____
☐	1	teaspoon cinnamon	_____
☐	¾	cup plain nonfat yogurt	_____
☐	2	teaspoons soy sauce	_____
☐	1	tablespoon Worcestershire sauce	_____
☐	1	tablespoon extra virgin olive oil	_____
☐	½	teaspoon brown sugar	_____
☐	½	teaspoon cayenne pepper	_____

1. Mix and blend beer, 2 tablespoons hot pepper sauce, salt, black pepper and cinnamon in a bowl to make marinade. Place wings in a re-sealable plastic bag. Pour beer mixture over wings, seal bag and refrigerate 3 hours. Turn bag several times while marinating.

2. Whisk yogurt, 2 tablespoons hot pepper sauce, soy sauce, Worcestershire, oil, and brown sugar together in a mixing bowl and blend well as a basting sauce. Taste, adjust flavoring. Refrigerate.

3. Place oven rack in middle position and preheat oven to 350°. Line a large jelly roll baking pan with aluminum foil and coat liberally with no-stick cooking spray.

4. Remove wings from beer marinade and place on pan. Baste wings with half of basting sauce and bake 20 minutes. Remove pan from oven and turn wings. Baste with remaining basting sauce and sprinkle lightly with cayenne pepper. Bake additional 10 – 20 minutes until done. Internal temperature of wings should be at least 165°.

5. Remove pan from oven, platter wings and cover with aluminum foil until ready to serve.

NOTES: Date: _____

RATE THIS RECIPE
○ ○ ○ ○ ○

BLOODY MARY ROASTED WINGS
Marinate | Oven

INGREDIENTS   SUBSTITUTIONS

- [ ] 12 wings segmented, tips discarded – rinsed/dried
- [ ] 1 cup spicy bloody mary mix _____
- [ ] 2 tablespoons lime juice _____
- [ ] 1 teaspoon Worcestershire sauce _____
- [ ] 1 tablespoon celery salt _____
- [ ] 2 teaspoons horseradish _____
- [ ] 1 teaspoon hot pepper sauce _____
- [ ] ½ teaspoon black pepper _____

1. Combine all ingredients except wings in a bowl and mix well. Taste, adjust flavoring. Place wings in a re-sealable plastic bag. Pour mixture into bag and seal. Refrigerate and marinate wings 3 hours. Turn bag several times while marinating.

2. Place oven rack in middle position and preheat oven to 350°. Line a large jelly roll baking pan with aluminum foil and coat liberally with no-stick cooking spray. Place wings on pan and cover with marinade.

3. Bake wings 20 minutes. Remove wings from oven, turn wings and baste with pan juices. Bake additional 10 – 20 minutes until done. Internal temperature of wings should be at least 165°.

4. Remove pan from oven, platter wings and cover with aluminum foil until ready to serve.

NOTES: Date: _____

RATE THIS RECIPE
○ ○ ○ ○ ○

BOURBON / MAPLE SYRUP WINGS

Oven

INGREDIENTS	SUBSTITUTIONS
☐ 12 wings segmented, tips discarded – rinsed/dried	
☐ 2 teaspoons black pepper	_____
☐ ½ teaspoons salt	_____
☐ ⅛ teaspoon cayenne pepper	_____
☐ 1 cup bourbon	_____
☐ 1 cup water	_____
☐ 3 tablespoons maple syrup	_____
☐ 2 teaspoons molasses	_____

1. Combine black pepper, salt and cayenne pepper in a large re-sealable plastic bag. Mix thoroughly. Add wings and toss to coat thoroughly.

2. Place oven rack in middle position. Preheat oven to 350º. Cover baking sheet with aluminum foil. Spray foil with no-stick cooking spray. Place wings on foil and bake 30 – 40 minutes or until done. Internal temperature of wings should be at least 165º.

3. Combine bourbon, water, maple syrup and molasses in a small saucepan over medium heat to make glaze. Bring to a boil. Reduce heat to simmer. Simmer 6 – 8 minutes until reduced by half. Add wings and glaze to large bowl and toss wings to coat thoroughly. Serve with blue cheese dip. See blue cheese dip recipes in appendix.

NOTES:

Date: _____

RATE THIS RECIPE
○ ○ ○ ○ ○

BRANDY / BROWN SUGAR WINGS
Oven

INGREDIENTS	SUBSTITUTIONS
☐ 12 wings segmented, tips discarded – rinsed/dried	
☐ ½ stick butter	_____
☐ 2 tablespoons Dijon mustard	_____
☐ 1½ cups brown sugar – packed	_____
☐ ½ cup soy sauce	_____
☐ 1 cup brandy	_____
☐ 1 teaspoon garlic cloves – minced	_____

1. Melt butter and mustard in a large skillet over medium heat. Add brown sugar, stir and cook until dissolved. Add soy sauce, brandy and garlic. Blend thoroughly.

2. Place oven rack in middle position. Preheat oven to 350°. Place wings in a large baking dish. Pour mixture over wings. Bake 35 – 45 minutes until wings are done. Baste frequently. Internal temperature of wings should be at least 165°.

3. Platter, wrap with foil and seal tightly until ready to serve.

NOTES:

Date: _____

RATE THIS RECIPE
○ ○ ○ ○ ○

A friend and I enjoy the occasional martini together, and it was during one of those social sessions that the possibility of a gin chicken wing recipe emerged from our discussions. You will find **GIN OVEN BAKED WINGS** on page 39.

I made the gin marinade several times before reaching the ultimate mixture. I started with ¼ cup of gin and a few juniper berries. After several "taste and adjust" sessions, I upped the gin to ½ cup and settled on a total of 12 crushed juniper berries. These changes produced the level of gin flavor I was seeking for the marinade. As a final touch, I added ginger and found that this addition provided a welcome twang.

As always, modify this – or any – recipe to suit your particular taste.

CITRUS JUICE WINGS

Oven

		INGREDIENTS	SUBSTITUTIONS
☐	12	wings segmented, tips discarded – rinsed/dried	
☐	1	tablespoon seasoned salt	_____
☐	½	teaspoon curry powder	_____
☐	½	teaspoon chili powder	_____
☐	½	teaspoon salt	_____
☐	½	teaspoon black pepper	_____
☐	1	cup orange juice	_____
☐	½	cup pineapple juice	_____
☐	½	cup white sugar	_____
☐	¼	cup soy sauce	_____
☐	¼	cup red wine	_____
☐	2	garlic cloves – minced	_____
☐	1	teaspoon onion powder	_____
☐	½	tablespoon ground ginger	_____
☐	1	tablespoon sesame oil	_____
☐	¼	teaspoon red pepper flakes – crushed	_____

1. Place oven rack in middle position and preheat oven to 350°. Line a large jelly roll baking pan with aluminum foil and coat liberally with no-stick cooking spray. Place wings in a large bowl and season wings with seasoned salt, curry powder, chili powder, salt and black pepper. Transfer wings to pan. Bake 20 minutes.

2. Combine remaining ingredients in a large skillet. Taste, adjust flavoring. Boil over medium-high heat stirring occasionally until reduced to a syrupy sauce, 10 – 12 minutes. Remove sauce from heat and cover to keep warm.

3. Remove pan from oven and spoon half of sauce evenly over wings. (Set aside other half of sauce for dipping.) Bake additional 10 – 20 minutes until done. Internal temperature of wings should be at least 165°.

4. Remove pan from oven, platter wings and cover with aluminum foil until ready to serve. Serve with set aside sauce for dipping.

NOTES: Date: _____

RATE THIS RECIPE
○ ○ ○ ○ ○

COFFEE LIQUEUR GRILLED WINGS
Marinate | Grill

	INGREDIENTS	SUBSTITUTIONS
☐ 12	wings segmented, tips discarded – rinsed/dried	
☐ ½	stick butter	_____
☐ 2	tablespoons dried onion – minced	_____
☐ 2	garlic cloves – minced	_____
☐ 1	teaspoon cumin	_____
☐ 1	teaspoon chili powder	_____
☐ ½	cup coffee liqueur	_____
☐ ½	teaspoon hot pepper sauce	_____
☐ 1	tablespoon barbecue sauce	_____
☐ 2	tablespoons Worcestershire sauce	_____
☐ 2	tablespoons soy sauce	_____
☐ 1	teaspoon black pepper	_____
☐ 2	tablespoons honey	_____

1. Melt butter in a saucepan over medium-direct heat, add onion and garlic and sauté until onions are wilted and translucent. Stir in cumin and chili powder and mix well. Add coffee liqueur and simmer mixture until reduced by half. Add hot pepper sauce, barbecue sauce, Worcestershire, soy sauce and pepper. Simmer 5 minutes. Remove saucepan from stove and mix in honey. Allow mixture to cool. Taste, adjust flavoring.

2. Place wings in a large re-sealable plastic bag. Pour marinade mixture into bag with wings, seal, refrigerate and marinate 3 hours. Turn bag several times while marinating to coat wings evenly.

3. Spray grill grates with no-stick cooking spray. Preheat grill for medium-direct heat. Place wings on grill. Grill wings on each side until done. Internal temperature of wings should be at least 165°.

4. Transfer wings from grill to a platter. Cover with aluminum foil until ready to serve.

NOTES: Date: _____

RATE THIS RECIPE
○ ○ ○ ○ ○

COLA OVEN BAKED WINGS

Oven

INGREDIENTS	SUBSTITUTIONS
☐ 12 wings segmented, tips discarded – rinsed/dried	
☐ 1 teaspoon garlic salt	_____
☐ ½ teaspoon celery salt	_____
☐ ½ teaspoon black pepper	_____
☐ ½ teaspoon onion powder	_____
☐ 1 can (12 ounce) cola	_____
☐ 1 cup brown sugar – packed	_____
☐ 2 tablespoons soy sauce	_____

1. Place oven rack in middle position and preheat oven to 350°. Place wings in a large baking dish. Combine garlic salt, celery salt, black pepper and onion powder in a bowl. Mix well. Season wings with mixture.

2. Combine cola, brown sugar and soy sauce in a medium bowl and mix well. Taste, adjust flavoring. Pour mixture over wings.

3. Bake wings covered 20 minutes. Remove dish from oven and turn wings. Baste with pan juices. Bake wings uncovered additional 10 – 20 minutes until done. Internal temperature of wings should be at least 165°.

4. Remove dish from oven, platter wings and cover with aluminum foil until ready to serve.

NOTES:

Date: _____

RATE THIS RECIPE
○ ○ ○ ○ ○

GIN OVEN BAKED WINGS

Marinate I Oven

		INGREDIENTS	SUBSTITUTIONS
☐	12	wings segmented, tips discarded – rinsed/dried	
☐	½	cup gin	_____
☐	4	tablespoons soy sauce	_____
☐	2	tablespoons white sugar	_____
☐	12	juniper berries – crushed fine	_____
☐	3	tablespoons water	_____
☐	½	teaspoon black pepper	_____
☐	¼	teaspoon ground ginger	_____

1. Combine all ingredients except wings in a re-sealable plastic bag and mix well for marinade. Taste, adjust flavoring. Add wings to bag, seal and marinate in refrigerator 3 hours. Turn bag several times while marinating.

2. Place oven rack in middle position and preheat oven to 350°. Line a large jelly roll baking pan with aluminum foil and coat liberally with no-stick cooking spray. Place wings on pan and spoon marinade over wings.

3. Bake 20 minutes. Remove pan from oven, turn wings and baste with pan juices. Bake additional 10 – 20 minutes until done. Internal temperature of wings should be at least 165°.

4. Remove pan from oven, platter wings and cover with aluminum foil until ready to serve.

NOTES: Date: _____

RATE THIS RECIPE
○ ○ ○ ○ ○

ORANGE JUICE / SHERRY WINGS
Oven

		INGREDIENTS	SUBSTITUTIONS
☐	12	wings segmented, tips discarded – rinsed/dried	
☐	½	cup fresh orange juice	_____
☐	½	cup sweet sherry	_____
☐	½	cup brown sugar – packed	_____
☐	¼	cup soy sauce	_____
☐	1	tablespoon Worcestershire sauce	_____
☐	2	tablespoons sesame oil	_____
☐	1	tablespoon lemon juice	_____
☐	2	teaspoons ground ginger	_____
☐	3	garlic cloves – minced	_____
☐	⅛	teaspoon red pepper flakes – crushed	_____
☐	3	tablespoons lime juice	_____

1. Place oven rack in middle position and preheat oven to 350°. Line a large jelly roll baking pan with aluminum foil. Coat foil liberally with no-stick cooking spray. Place wings on pan. Bake 20 minutes.

2. Combine all remaining ingredients except lime juice in a medium saucepan. Boil over medium heat, stirring occasionally until sauce thickens, 8 – 10 minutes. Add lime juice. Mix thoroughly. Taste, adjust flavoring.

3. Remove wings from oven and spoon sauce over wings. Bake additional 10 – 20 minutes until done. Internal temperature of wings should be at least 165°.

4. Remove pan from oven, platter wings and cover with aluminum foil until ready to serve.

NOTES: Date: _____

RATE THIS RECIPE
○ ○ ○ ○ ○

RED WINE / CURRANT JELLY GLAZED WINGS
Marinate | Oven

INGREDIENTS   SUBSTITUTIONS

- [ ] 12 wings segmented, tips discarded – rinsed/dried
- [ ] ¼ cup soy sauce   _____
- [ ] ¼ cup orange juice   _____
- [ ] ½ cup dry red wine   _____
- [ ] 3 garlic cloves – finely minced   _____
- [ ] 2 tablespoons ginger root – chopped   _____
- [ ] 6 tablespoons red currant jelly   _____
- [ ] 2 tablespoons orange zest   _____

1. Combine soy sauce, orange juice, red wine, garlic and ginger root in a large re-sealable plastic bag and mix thoroughly. Add wings and toss to coat well. Seal bag and refrigerate 3 hours.

2. Combine jelly and orange zest. Stir and mix vigorously until jelly is nearly liquefied. Set aside.

3. Place oven rack in middle position. Preheat oven to 350°. Cover baking sheet with aluminum foil. Spray foil with no-stick cooking spray. Place wings on baking sheet. Bake 20 minutes. Baste wings liberally with jelly sauce. Bake aditional10 minutes. Turn wings and baste with jelly sauce. Bake wings until done. Internal temperature of wings should be at least 165º.

4. Remove pan from oven, platter wings and cover with aluminum foil until ready to serve.

NOTES: Date: _____

RATE THIS RECIPE
○ ○ ○ ○ ○

RED WINE / SOY SAUCE WINGS
Marinate | Oven

INGREDIENTS   SUBSTITUTIONS

- [ ] 12   wings segmented, tips discarded – rinsed/dried
- [ ] ¼   cup red wine   _____
- [ ] ¼   cup soy sauce   _____
- [ ] ¼   cup extra virgin olive oil   _____
- [ ] ½   teaspoon ground cinnamon   _____
- [ ] ¼   teaspoon ground cloves   _____
- [ ] ¼   teaspoon allspice   _____
- [ ] ¼   teaspoon black pepper   _____

1. Combine all ingredients except wings in a large re-sealable plastic bag and mix thoroughly. Taste, adjust flavoring. Add wings to bag, seal and refrigerate 3 hours. Turn bag occasionally to coat wings thoroughly.

2. Place oven rack in middle position and preheat oven to 350°. Line a large jelly roll pan with aluminum foil and coat liberally with no-stick cooking spray. Place wings on pan. Spoon some marinade over wings. Discard bag and remaining marinade.

3. Bake 20 minutes. Remove pan from oven, turn wings and baste with pan juices. Bake additional 10 – 20 minutes until done. Internal temperature of wings should be at least 165°. Remove pan from oven, platter wings and cover with aluminum foil until ready to serve. Serve with blue cheese dip. See blue cheese dip recipes in appendix.

NOTES: Date: _____

RATE THIS RECIPE
○ ○ ○ ○ ○

RED WINE WINGS

Stove Top | Broil

	INGREDIENTS	SUBSTITUTIONS
☐	12 wings segmented, tips discarded – rinsed/dried	
☐	1 cup red wine	_____
☐	¼ cup soy sauce	_____
☐	¼ cup brown sugar – packed	_____
☐	1 tablespoon hoisin sauce	_____
☐	2 teaspoons ground cinnamon	_____
☐	2 garlic cloves – minced	_____
☐	¼ teaspoon red chili flakes – crushed	_____
☐	1½ tablespoons ground ginger	_____
☐	½ teaspoon onion salt	_____

1. Combine all ingredients except wings in a large skillet and mix well. Taste, adjust flavoring. Bring mixture to a boil. Reduce heat to a low simmer.

2. Add wings to skillet. Simmer on low 1 – 1½ hours until nearly all of sauce evaporates and forms a glaze on wings and wings are done. Internal temperature of wings should be at least 165°. To obtain a crisp exterior on wings, broil in oven 4 – 6 minutes.

3. Remove pan from oven, platter wings and cover with aluminum foil until ready to serve. Serve with blue cheese dip. See blue cheese dip recipes in appendix.

NOTES: Date: _____

RATE THIS RECIPE
○ ○ ○ ○ ○

ROOT BEER / HOT SAUCE WINGS

Grill

		INGREDIENTS	SUBSTITUTIONS
☐	12	wings segmented, tips discarded – rinsed/dried	
☐	1	can (12 ounce) root beer	_____
☐	½	cup hot pepper sauce	_____
☐	½	teaspoon cayenne pepper	_____
☐	¼	teaspoon black pepper	_____
☐	3	tablespoons lemon juice	_____
☐	1	tablespoon soy sauce	_____

1. Mix together all ingredients except wings in a large skillet. Taste, adjust flavoring. Add wings to skillet. Simmer on stove top 10 minutes.

2. Prepare grill to medium-direct heat.

3. Remove wings from sauce and place on grill 6 – 8 minutes. Turn wings frequently to avoid burning. Return wings to sauce in skillet and place skillet on grill. Simmer 5 minutes.

4. Transfer wings to grill and grill until done. Turn wings to avoid burning. Continue simmering sauce on grill while wings are cooking. Internal temperature of wings should be at least 165°.

5. Transfer wings from grill to a platter. Spoon sauce over wings. Cover with aluminum foil until ready to serve.

NOTES:

Date: _____

RATE THIS RECIPE
○ ○ ○ ○ ○

SHERRY / OYSTER SAUCE WINGS

Marinate I Oven

	INGREDIENTS	SUBSTITUTIONS
☐	12 wings segmented, tips discarded – rinsed/dried	
☐	½ teaspoon salt – divided	_____
☐	½ teaspoon black pepper – divided	_____
☐	4 tablespoons soy sauce	_____
☐	4 tablespoons oyster sauce	_____
☐	4 tablespoons sweet sherry	_____
☐	¾ cup all-purpose flour	_____
☐	¾ cup fine bread crumbs	_____

1. Season wings with ¼ teaspoon salt and ¼ teaspoon black pepper. Place wings in a large re-sealable plastic bag. Mix soy sauce, oyster sauce, sherry, ¼ teaspoon salt and ¼ teaspoon black pepper in a bowl and blend thoroughly. Taste, adjust flavoring. Pour mixture into bag and shake bag to coat wings well. Seal bag and refrigerate 3 hours.

2. Mix flour and fine bread crumbs in a large bowl. Dredge marinated wings in flour/bread crumb mixture until well coated.

3. Place oven rack in middle position and preheat oven to 350°. Line a large jelly roll pan with aluminum foil and coat liberally with no-stick cooking spray. Place wings on pan. Spoon some marinade on wings. Discard bag and remaining marinade.

4. Bake wings 20 minutes. Remove from oven, turn wings and baste with any pan juices. Bake additional 10 – 20 minutes until done. Internal temperature of wings should be at least 165°.

NOTES: Date: _____

RATE THIS RECIPE
○ ○ ○ ○ ○

SHERRY / SOY SAUCE / BROWN SUGAR WINGS
Oven

		INGREDIENTS	SUBSTITUTIONS
☐	12	wings segmented, tips discarded – rinsed/dried	
☐	3	teaspoons dry sherry	_____
☐	½	cup soy sauce	_____
☐	½	cup brown sugar – packed	_____
☐	1	tablespoon onion – minced	_____
☐	3	garlic cloves – minced	_____
☐	½	tablespoon smoked paprika	_____
☐	1	teaspoon ground ginger	_____
☐	1	teaspoon cider vinegar	_____
☐	½	teaspoon black pepper	_____

1. Place oven rack in middle position and preheat oven to 350°. Place wings in a large shallow baking dish.

2. In a food blender, combine and blend remaining ingredients. Taste, adjust flavoring. Pour mixture over wings and toss to coat thoroughly.

3. Bake wings in oven 20 minutes. Remove dish from oven, turn wings and baste with dish juices. Bake additional 10 – 20 minutes until done. Internal temperature of wings should be at least 165°.

4. Remove dish from oven. Remove wings with a slotted spoon.

NOTES:

Date: _____

RATE THIS RECIPE
○ ○ ○ ○ ○

SPICED RUM / ONION WINGS

Marinate I Oven

INGREDIENTS	SUBSTITUTIONS
☐ 12 wings segmented, tips discarded – rinsed/dried	
☐ ½ cup spiced rum	_____
☐ ½ teaspoon salt	_____
☐ ½ teaspoon black pepper	_____
☐ 1 garlic clove – minced	_____
☐ 2 teaspoons dried rosemary	_____
☐ 1 teaspoon paprika	_____
☐ 3 tablespoons extra virgin olive oil	_____
☐ 3 medium onions – thinly sliced	_____

1. Pour spiced rum into a large re-sealable plastic bag. Add wings, seal and refrigerator 3 hours. Turn bag several times while marinating.

2. Combine salt, black pepper, garlic, rosemary, paprika and oil in a bowl for seasoning mixture. Taste, adjust flavoring.

3. Place oven rack in middle position and preheat oven to 350°. Line a large jelly roll baking pan with aluminum foil and coat liberally with no-stick cooking spray. Place wings on pan. Dab and brush wings with seasoning mixture. Spoon some rum over wings and discard remaining rum. Distribute half of sliced onions over wings.

4. Bake 20 minutes. Remove wings from oven and turn and baste with pan juices. Distribute remaining half of onions over wings and bake additional 10 – 20 minutes until done. Internal temperature of wings should be at least 165°.

5. Remove pan from oven, platter wings and cover with aluminum foil until ready to serve.

NOTES:

Date: _____

RATE THIS RECIPE
○ ○ ○ ○ ○

STOUT BEER / BARBECUE SAUCE WINGS
Stove Top | Broil

	INGREDIENTS	SUBSTITUTIONS
☐ 12	wings segmented, tips discarded – rinsed/dried	
☐ ¾	cup hot pepper sauce	_____
☐ 1	bottle (12 ounce) stout beer	_____
☐ 2	cups spicy barbecue sauce	_____
☐ 2	tablespoons water	_____

1. Combine wings with hot pepper sauce and beer in large saucepan. Bring to a boil and reduce heat to simmer. Simmer 20 minutes.

2. Mix barbecue sauce with water. Dip wings in mixture.

3. Place oven rack in broil position. Preheat broiler. Cover large rimmed baking sheet with aluminum foil. Spray foil with no-stick cooking spray. Spread wings and sauce on sheet. Broil 6 minutes. Turn wings and broil until done. Internal temperature of wings should be at least 165°. Serve with blue cheese dip. See blue cheese dip recipes in appendix.

NOTES: Date: _____

RATE THIS RECIPE
○ ○ ○ ○ ○

The **SHERRY / SOY SAUCE / SUGAR WINGS** recipe on page 46 is a personal favorite. I've made numerous modifications to the recipe which was, at first, primarily a soy sauce and brown sugar affair.

The acidity in the dry sherry, cider vinegar and soy sauce in contrast with the sweetness in the onion, garlic and brown sugar creates a flavor profile that, for my palate, is immensely satisfying.

This recipe is a great example of the rewards you can reap through experimentation.

TEQUILA / CHIPOTLE WINGS
Marinate | Deep Fry

		INGREDIENTS	SUBSTITUTIONS
☐	12	wings segmented, tips discarded – rinsed/dried	
☐	½	cup orange juice	_____
☐	½	cup lime juice	_____
☐	½	cup agave nectar	_____
☐	¼	cup tequila	_____
☐	¼	cup chopped cilantro	_____
☐	4	garlic cloves – minced	_____
☐	2	teaspoons salt – divided	_____
☐	1	chipotle pepper – minced	_____
☐	4	tablespoons butter	_____
☐	1	teaspoon hot pepper sauce	_____
☐	2	tablespoons garlic powder	_____
☐	1	tablespoon black pepper	_____
☐	1	tablespoon ground cumin	_____
☐	1	teaspoon liquid smoke	_____
☐		canola oil or peanut oil for deep frying	_____

1. Combine orange juice, lime juice, agave nectar, tequila, cilantro, garlic, 1 teaspoon salt and chipotle in a food processor. Taste, adjust flavoring. Pour processed mixture into a saucepan and bring to a boil. Reduce heat to medium low and cook until sauce is reduced by half and thickened. Melt butter into mixture. Taste, adjust flavoring. Set aside.

2. Mix 1 teaspoon salt and all other ingredients except wings and canola oil in a large mixing bowl and mix thoroughly. Set aside in a large bowl.

3. Add enough oil to a heavy skillet or deep fryer to cover wings. Heat oil to 375°. Add wings and cook until done. Internal temperature of wings should be at least 165°. Drain wings on paper towels. Plunge wings into set aside sauce and toss to coat completely. Serve with blue cheese dip. See dip recipes in appendix.

NOTES: Date: _____

RATE THIS RECIPE
○ ○ ○ ○ ○

TEQUILA / CITRUS WINGS
Marinate | Oven | Broil

INGREDIENTS   SUBSTITUTIONS

- [ ] 12 wings segmented, tips discarded – rinsed/dried
- [ ] ½ cup tequila
- [ ] ¼ cup orange juice
- [ ] ¼ cup lime juice
- [ ] ½ cup cilantro – chopped
- [ ] 2 tablespoons extra virgin olive oil
- [ ] ½ tablespoon black pepper
- [ ] 3 garlic cloves – minced
- [ ] 2 teaspoons hot pepper sauce
- [ ] 1 teaspoon grated orange zest
- [ ] 1 teaspoon grated lime zest
- [ ] 1 orange peel – julienne (garnish)
- [ ] 2 limes – sliced wedges (garnish)

1.   Combine all ingredients except orange peel and lime wedges in a large re-sealable plastic bag and mix thoroughly. Taste, adjust flavoring. Add wings and toss to coat thoroughly. Seal bag and refrigerate 3 hours. Turn bag to coat wings evenly.

2.   Place one oven rack in middle position. Place a second rack in broil position. Preheat oven to 400°. Cover baking sheet with aluminum foil. Spray foil with no-stick cooking spray. Place wings on foil. Bake wings 30 minutes on lower rack

3.   Pour marinade from bag into a saucepan, bring to a boil and simmer 6 – 8 minutes until reduced by half. Set aside.

4.   Remove wings from oven. Preheat broiler. Brush wings with marinade and broil wings 4 – 6 minutes until crisp and done. Turn and baste wings at least once while broiling. Internal temperature of wings should be at least 165°.

5.   Garnish with orange peel and lime wedges.

NOTES: Date: _____

RATE THIS RECIPE
○ ○ ○ ○ ○

TEQUILA / LIME WINGS

Marinate | Oven | Broil

INGREDIENTS   SUBSTITUTIONS

- [ ] 12 wings segmented, tips discarded – rinsed/dried
- [ ] ½ stick butter   _____
- [ ] ½ cup tequila   _____
- [ ] ⅓ cup green salsa   _____
- [ ] 1 tablespoon green hot pepper sauce   _____
- [ ] 3 tablespoons lime juice   _____
- [ ] ½ teaspoon red pepper flakes – crushed   _____
- [ ] 2 green onions – chopped   _____
- [ ] ¼ cup cilantro – no stems/chopped   _____
- [ ] ½ teaspoon pepper   _____

1. Melt butter in a large saucepan. Add all other ingredients except wings to saucepan. Bring to a simmer. Taste, adjust flavorings. Cool. Place wings in a re-sealable plastic bag. Pour butter mixture into bag with wings. Seal bag, and refrigerate wings 3 hours. Turn bag occasionally.

2. Place one oven rack in middle position and a second rack in broil position. Preheat oven to 350°. Transfer wings and mixture to a large shallow dish. Bake 20 minutes on lower rack, turn wings and baste with dish juices. Bake additional 10 minutes.

3. Remove dish from oven and baste wings with dish juices. Line a large jelly pan with aluminum foil and coat foil with no-stick cooking spray. Preheat oven to broil. Transfer wings to pan and broil until done. Internal temperature of wings should be at least 165°.

4. Remove pan from oven, platter wings and cover with aluminum foil until ready to serve.

NOTES: Date: _____

RATE THIS RECIPE
○ ○ ○ ○ ○

VODKA WINGS

Oven

	INGREDIENTS	SUBSTITUTIONS
☐	12 wings segmented, tips discarded – rinsed/dried	
☐	½ cup vodka	_____
☐	½ cup soy sauce	_____
☐	½ cup ketchup	_____
☐	½ cup honey	_____
☐	3 garlic cloves – minced	_____

1. Place all ingredients except wings in a re-sealable plastic bag and mix thoroughly. Add wings to bag. Seal bag and marinate wings in refrigerator 3 hours, turning occasionally while refrigerating to coat evenly.

2. Place oven rack in middle position. Preheat oven to 350°. Line a large baking pan with aluminum foil and spray with no-stick cooking spray. Place wings on baking pan. Spoon marinade over wings. Bake wings, basting occasionally with pan juices, 35 – 45 minutes until done. Turn once while baking and baste with pan juices. Internal temperature of wings should be at least 165°.

4. Remove pan from oven, platter wings and cover with aluminum foil until ready to serve.

NOTES:

Date: _____

RATE THIS RECIPE
○ ○ ○ ○ ○

WHISKEY / HOT SAUCE DEEP FRIED WINGS

Deep Fry

		INGREDIENTS	SUBSTITUTIONS
☐	12	wings segmented, tips discarded – rinsed/dried	
☐	1	cup all-purpose flour	_____
☐	2	teaspoons lemon pepper seasoning	_____
☐	2	teaspoons rosemary – finely chopped	_____
☐	1	teaspoon Cajun seasoning salt	_____
☐	1	teaspoon ground garlic clove	_____
☐	3	eggs	_____
☐	1	cup milk	_____
☐		canola oil or peanut oil for deep frying	_____
☐	½	cup whiskey	_____
☐	½	stick butter	_____
☐	½	cup hot pepper sauce	_____
☐	1	tablespoon Worcestershire sauce	_____

1. Combine flour, lemon pepper, rosemary, Cajun seasoning salt and garlic in a large re-sealable plastic bag. In a bowl, blend eggs and milk. Add wings and coat well. Place wings in bag and toss to coat.

2. Place enough oil in a heavy skillet or deep fryer to cover wings. Heat oil to 350º. Add wings and cook until done. Internal temperature of wings should be at least 165º.

3. Melt butter in a saucepan. Cool. Add whiskey, butter, hot sauce and Worcestershire in a large bowl and mix thoroughly. Add wings and toss to coat thoroughly. Serve with blue cheese dip. See blue cheese dip recipes in appendix.

NOTES: Date: _____

RATE THIS RECIPE
○ ○ ○ ○ ○

I find shopping for ingredients to be a great deal of fun. I frequent many area grocery stores and meat markets, always searching for the freshest ingredients and the best bargains. Getting to know the wonderful people that staff these establishments has been a fantastic side benefit of my frequent visits.

For ingredients I use all the time, I purchase the largest amounts possible—large ketchup bottles, big jars of mustard, 64 ounce jugs of vinegar and enormous bottles of soy sauce. And I've learned that "on sale" ingredients, especially meats, are sometimes not the best they can be. Choose your ingredients carefully!

WHISKEY / ORANGE JUICE WINGS
Grill | Deep Fry

		INGREDIENTS	SUBSTITUTIONS
☐	12	wings segmented, tips discarded – rinsed/dried	
☐	½	cup hickory wood chips	_____
☐	¼	cup whiskey	_____
☐	¾	cup orange juice	_____
☐	½	cup ketchup	_____
☐	1	tablespoon onion powder	_____
☐	1	tablespoon garlic powder	_____
☐	¼	teaspoon cayenne pepper	_____
☐	1	tablespoon Worcestershire sauce	_____
☐	¼	cup soy sauce	_____
☐	¼	cup hot pepper sauce	_____
☐	¼	cup cider vinegar	_____
☐	¼	cup brown sugar	_____
☐	1	stick butter	_____
☐		canola oil or peanut oil for deep frying	_____

1. Spray grill grate with no-stick cooking spray. Prepare grill for low-indirect heat. Wings should not be placed directly over heat. Sprinkle hickory chips on coals. Grill wings 20 minutes.

2. Add all other ingredients except wings and oil to a saucepan. Bring to a boil. Reduce heat and simmer 15 minutes. Taste, adjust flavoring. Set aside in a large bowl.

3. Add enough oil to a heavy skillet or deep fryer to cover wings. Heat oil to 375°. Remove wings from grill and place in skillet or deep fryer. Cook wings until done. Internal temperature of wings should be at least 165°. Drain wings on paper towels. Plunge wings into set aside sauce and toss to coat completely.

NOTES: Date: _____

RATE THIS RECIPE
○ ○ ○ ○ ○

WHISKEY MARINADED WINGS

Marinate | Oven

INGREDIENTS	SUBSTITUTIONS
☐ 12 wings segmented, tips discarded – rinsed/dried	
☐ ½ stick butter	_____
☐ ½ teaspoon corn starch	_____
☐ ⅓ cup brown sugar – packed	_____
☐ ¼ teaspoon garlic powder	_____
☐ ½ teaspoon ginger powder	_____
☐ ¼ cup soy sauce	_____
☐ ¾ cup whiskey	_____
☐ 1 tablespoon ketchup	_____

1. Melt butter in a small skillet. Combine all other ingredients except wings in a bowl and blend until smooth. Add butter to bowl and mix well.

2. Place wings in a re-sealable plastic bag. Add mixture to bag. Seal bag and marinate wings in refrigerator 3 hours. Turn bag occasionally.

3. Place oven rack in middle position and preheat oven to 350°. Line a large jelly roll baking pan with aluminum foil and coat with no-stick cooking spray. Arrange wings on pan. Spoon some marinade over wings.

4. Bake wings 20 minutes. Remove pan from oven, turn wings and baste with pan juices. Bake additional 10 – 20 minutes until done. Internal temperature of wings should be at least 165°.

5. Remove pan from oven, platter wings and cover with aluminum foil until ready to serve.

NOTES: Date: _____

RATE THIS RECIPE
○ ○ ○ ○ ○

WHISKEY / RED WINE WINGS
Marinate I Oven

		INGREDIENTS	SUBSTITUTIONS
☐	12	wings segmented, tips discarded – rinsed/dried	
☐	½	cup soy sauce	
☐	¾	cup brown sugar – packed	_____
☐	½	teaspoon garlic powder	_____
☐	1	teaspoon ground ginger	_____
☐	½	teaspoon onion powder	_____
☐	1	cup whiskey	_____
☐	4	tablespoons red wine	_____

1. In a large bowl, combine soy sauce, brown sugar, garlic powder, ginger, onion and whiskey. Stir and mix until smooth. Taste, adjust flavoring.

2. Place wings in a re-sealable plastic bag. Add whiskey mixture to bag. Seal bag and marinate in refrigerator 3 hours turning occasionally.

3. Place oven rack in middle position and preheat oven to 350°. Line a large jelly roll baking pan with aluminum foil. Coat foil with no-stick cooking spray. Place wings on pan. Spoon some marinade over wings.

4. Bake 20 minutes. Remove pan from oven, turn wings and baste with pan juices. Drizzle red wine over wings. Bake additional 10 – 20 minutes until done. Internal temperature of wings should be at least 165°.

5. Remove pan from oven, platter wings and cover with aluminum foil until ready to serve.

NOTES: Date: _____

RATE THIS RECIPE
○ ○ ○ ○ ○

FRUIT WINGS

One of my great joys in creating this cookbook has been lavishing careful attention on the clarity of the step-by-step cooking instructions. Too many times I've attempted to prepare a "new-to-me" recipe and found that the instructions were confusing at best, and, at worst, downright detrimental to the finished product.

With this cookbook, every effort has been made to clearly document each step in the cooking process and to present those steps in a no-nonsense manner that facilitates a successful outcome.

Always read a recipe all the way through before beginning, confirming that it makes sense to you, and that you have the ingredients and cooking tools you'll need. I hope you agree that our persnickety emphasis on clarity has been worth the effort.

APRICOT PRESERVES / DIJON WINGS

Oven

	INGREDIENTS	SUBSTITUTIONS
☐	12 wings segmented, tips discarded – rinsed/dried	
☐	1 cup apricot preserves	_____
☐	2 tablespoons brown sugar	_____
☐	½ teaspoon celery salt	_____
☐	1 teaspoon dry mustard	_____
☐	½ teaspoon ground ginger	_____
☐	¼ cup cider vinegar	_____
☐	⅓ cup Dijon mustard	_____
☐	2 tablespoons extra virgin olive oil	_____
☐	1 tablespoon water	_____
☐	½ teaspoon salt	_____
☐	½ teaspoon black pepper	_____

1. Prepare sauce by combining apricot preserves, brown sugar, celery salt, dry mustard, ginger and vinegar in a small saucepan over medium heat until brown sugar is dissolved and mixture is well blended. Taste, adjust flavoring.

2. Combine Dijon mustard, oil, water, salt and black pepper in a large bowl. Add wings to Dijon mustard mixture and stir to coat.

3. Place oven rack in middle position and preheat oven to 350°. Line a large jelly roll baking pan with aluminum foil and coat liberally with no-stick cooking spray. Place coated wings on pan and spoon half of apricot mixture over wings.

4. Bake 20 minutes. Remove pan, turn wings and baste with remaining apricot sauce. Return wings to oven and bake additional 10 – 20 minutes until done. Internal temperature of wings should be at least 165°.

5. Remove pan from oven, platter wings and cover with aluminum foil until ready to serve.

NOTES: Date: _____

RATE THIS RECIPE
○ ○ ○ ○ ○

APRICOT PRESERVES / DRIED ONION SOUP WINGS

Oven

	INGREDIENTS	SUBSTITUTIONS
☐	12 wings segmented, tips discarded – rinsed/dried	
☐	1 cup apricot preserves	_____
☐	1 package (1.25 ounce) dry onion soup mix	_____
☐	½ cup ketchup	_____
☐	⅓ cup extra virgin olive oil	_____
☐	⅓ cup white sugar	_____
☐	⅓ cup cider vinegar	_____
☐	¼ teaspoon paprika	_____
☐	⅛ teaspoon garlic powder	_____

1. Place oven rack in middle position and preheat oven to 350°. Line a large jelly roll baking pan with aluminum foil and coat liberally with no-stick cooking spray. Place wings on pan. Spoon and spread apricot preserves equally over wings. Spoon and sprinkle dry onion soup mix equally over apricot preserves on wings.

2. Combine last six ingredients in a mixing bowl and blend well. Taste, adjust flavoring. Spoon mixture evenly over onion soup mix, preserves and wings.

3. Bake in oven 20 minutes. Remove wings from oven. Spoon pan juices over wings without disturbing onion soup mix and preserves on wings. Bake additional 10 – 20 minutes until done. Internal temperature of wings should be at least 165°.

4. Remove pan from oven, platter wings and cover with aluminum foil until ready to serve.

NOTES: Date: _____

RATE THIS RECIPE
○ ○ ○ ○ ○

BANANA / GREEN CHILIES WINGS
Grill

INGREDIENTS	SUBSTITUTIONS
☐ 12 wings segmented, tips discarded – rinsed/dried	
☐ 1 can (4 ounce) diced green chilies – drained	_____
☐ ¼ cup onion – chopped	_____
☐ 2 tablespoons apricot preserves	_____
☐ 1 tablespoon brown sugar	_____
☐ 1 tablespoon lemon juice	_____
☐ ½ tablespoon fish sauce	_____
☐ ½ teaspoon ground allspice	_____
☐ 1 large banana – peeled/diced	_____
☐ ½ teaspoon salt	_____
☐ ½ teaspoon black pepper	_____

1. Purée chilies, onion, apricot preserves, brown sugar, lemon juice, fish sauce, allspice and banana in a blender to create dip. Taste, adjust flavoring. Season sauce with salt and black pepper to taste. Thicken sauce by simmering over low heat in a small saucepan 10 minutes. Set aside.

2. Spray grill grates with no-stick cooking spray. Prepare grill to medium-direct heat. Grill wings until done. Turn wings frequently to avoid burning. Internal temperature of wings should be at least 165°. Sprinkle wings lightly with salt and black pepper.

3. Transfer wings from grill to a platter. Cover with aluminum foil until ready to serve.

4. Serve dip sauce with wings.

NOTES: Date: _____

RATE THIS RECIPE
○ ○ ○ ○ ○

GRAPEFRUIT JUICE WINGS

Oven

	INGREDIENTS	SUBSTITUTIONS
☐	12 wings segmented, tips discarded – rinsed/dried	
☐	2 tablespoons extra virgin olive oil	_____
☐	½ teaspoon salt	_____
☐	½ teaspoon black pepper	_____
☐	1 cup grapefruit juice	_____
☐	½ cup soy sauce	_____
☐	½ cup hoisin sauce	_____
☐	¼ cup ketchup	_____
☐	2 tablespoons white wine vinegar	_____
☐	¼ cup brown sugar	_____
☐	1 teaspoon hot pepper sauce	_____
☐	1 garlic clove – minced	_____
☐	1 tablespoon ground ginger	_____

1. Put wings in a bowl, drizzle with oil and season well with salt and black pepper. Toss to evenly season wings.

2. Combine remaining ingredients in a large saucepan. Taste, adjust flavoring. Simmer mixture over low heat until slightly thickened.

3. Line a large jelly roll pan with aluminum foil and coat liberally with no-stick cooking spray. Place wings in a single layer on baking sheet. Place oven rack in middle position and preheat oven to 350°. Bake wings 20 minutes. Turn wings and bake additional 10 – 20 minutes until done. Internal temperature of wings should be at least 165°.

4. When wings are done, add them to saucepan and simmer 5 or more minutes. Remove wings with a slotted spoon. Serve with blue cheese dip. See blue cheese dip recipes in appendix.

NOTES: Date: _____

RATE THIS RECIPE
○ ○ ○ ○ ○

GRAPEFRUIT JUICE GRILLED WINGS
Marinate | Grill

INGREDIENTS	SUBSTITUTIONS
☐ 12 wings segmented, tips discarded – rinsed/dried	
☐ ⅓ cup soy sauce	_____
☐ ½ cup grapefruit juice	_____
☐ ½ cup sesame seeds	_____
☐ 3 tablespoons hoisin sauce	_____
☐ 2 tablespoons ketchup	_____
☐ 3 tablespoons cider vinegar	_____
☐ 3 tablespoons brown sugar	_____
☐ 3 garlic cloves – minced	_____
☐ 2 tablespoons ground ginger	_____

1. Place wings in a re-sealable plastic bag. Blend all other ingredients in a bowl and mix well. Taste, adjust flavoring. Reserve a quarter of mixture in a bowl, cover and set aside in refrigerator. Reserved marinade is to be use for basting while grilling. Pour remaining three-quarters marinade over wings. Seal bag and refrigerate 3 hours. Turn bag several times while marinating to coat wings evenly.

2. Spray grill grates with no-stick cooking spray. Prepare grill to medium-high heat. Remove wings from bag and place wings on grill. Grill wings until done. Turn wings and baste frequently with set aside marinade. Internal temperature of wings should be at least 165°.

3. Transfer wings from grill to a platter. Cover with aluminum foil until ready to serve.

NOTES: Date: _____

RATE THIS RECIPE
○ ○ ○ ○ ○

LEMON JUICE / DIJON GRILLED WINGS
Marinate | Grill

	INGREDIENTS	SUBSTITUTIONS
☐ 12	wings segmented, tips discarded – rinsed/dried	
☐ 2	tablespoons lemon juice	_____
☐ 2	tablespoons Dijon mustard	_____
☐ ¼	cup extra virgin olive oil	_____
☐ 1	teaspoon lemon zest	_____
☐ 3	garlic cloves – minced	_____
☐ 1	teaspoon paprika	_____
☐ ½	teaspoon salt	_____
☐ ½	tablespoon pepper	_____

1. In a large bowl, stir together all ingredients except wings and mix thoroughly. Taste, adjust flavoring. Place a quarter of sauce in a bowl, cover and set aside in refrigerator. Reserved marinade is to be use for basting while grilling. Place wings in a re-sealable plastic bag. Pour remaining three-quarters sauce over wings, seal bag and marinate in refrigerator 3 hours. Turn bag occasionally to marinate wings evenly.

2. Spray grill grates with no-stick cooking spray. Prepare grill to medium-high direct heat. Grill wings until done. Turn and baste frequently with set aside sauce. Internal temperature of wings should be at least 165°.

3. Transfer wings from grill to a platter. Cover with aluminum foil until ready to serve..

NOTES:

Date: _____

RATE THIS RECIPE
○ ○ ○ ○ ○

LEMON JUICE / SOY SAUCE WINGS

Marinate | Grill | Broil

		INGREDIENTS	SUBSTITUTIONS
☐	12	wings segmented, tips discarded – rinsed/dried	
☐	½	cup lemon juice	_____
☐	¼	cup soy sauce	_____
☐	¼	cup vegetable oil	_____
☐	3	tablespoons chili sauce	_____
☐	1	garlic clove – finely chopped	_____
☐	¼	teaspoon black pepper	_____
☐	¼	teaspoon celery seed	_____
☐	¼	teaspoon ground ginger	_____
☐	¼	teaspoon garlic powder	_____
☐	¼	teaspoon dry mustard	_____
☐	2	lemons – sliced (garnish)	_____

1. Combine lemon juice, soy sauce, vegetable oil, chili sauce, garlic, black pepper, celery seed, ginger, garlic and mustard in a large re-sealable plastic bag. Mix well. Add wings to bag. Seal bag, marinate and refrigerate for 3 hours.

2. Place one oven rack in middle position and another oven rack in broiler position. Preheat oven to 350°. Line a large jelly roll pan with aluminum foil and coat liberally with no-stick cooking spray. Place wings on baking pan and spoon marinade over wings. Place pan on middle rack and bake wings 20 minutes.

3. Remove wings from middle position, turn wings and baste with pan juices. Increase heat to broil. Place pan in broil position and broil 5 minutes on each side until done. Internal temperature of wings should be at least 165°. Garnish with lemon wedges.

NOTES: Date: _____

RATE THIS RECIPE
○ ○ ○ ○ ○

LIME / HOT SAUCE WINGS

Marinate | Oven

INGREDIENTS	SUBSTITUTIONS
☐ 12 wings segmented, tips discarded – rinsed/dried	
☐ ¼ cup lime juice	_____
☐ ¼ cup extra virgin olive oil	_____
☐ 2 teaspoons hot pepper sauce	_____
☐ ½ cup cornmeal	_____
☐ ½ cup all-purpose flour	_____
☐ ½ teaspoon salt	_____
☐ ½ teaspoon ground cumin	_____
☐ ½ teaspoon black pepper	_____

1. Combine lime juice, oil and hot pepper sauce in a large re-sealable plastic bag and mix well. Taste, adjust flavoring. Add wings, seal bag and toss to coat wings thoroughly. Seal and refrigerate 3 hours. Turn occasionally.

2. Place oven rack in middle position and preheat oven to 350°. Line a large jelly roll baking pan with aluminum foil and coat with a no-stick cooking spray. Combine cornmeal, flour, salt, cumin and black pepper in another large re-sealable plastic bag. Place wings in bag and shake to coat thoroughly.

3. Shake excess coating off wings and place on pan. Bake 25 minutes, turn wings and baste with any pan juices. Bake additional 25 – 35 minutes until done. Internal temperature of wings should be at least 165°.

4. Remove pan from oven, platter wings and cover with aluminum foil until ready to serve.

NOTES: Date: _____

RATE THIS RECIPE
○ ○ ○ ○ ○

ORANGE JUICE / BUTTER BREADED WINGS

Oven

	INGREDIENTS	SUBSTITUTIONS
☐	12 wings segmented, tips discarded – rinsed/dried	
☐	½ cup all-purpose flour	_____
☐	½ cup dry bread crumbs – fine	_____
☐	¼ teaspoon salt	_____
☐	½ teaspoon black pepper	_____
☐	½ teaspoon celery salt	_____
☐	2 eggs – beaten	_____
☐	¼ stick butter	_____
☐	1 onion – chopped	_____
☐	¼ cup orange juice	_____
☐	¼ cup ketchup	_____
☐	1 tablespoon brown sugar	_____
☐	1 tablespoon soy sauce	_____
☐	¼ teaspoon ground ginger	_____
☐	1 teaspoon garlic salt	_____

1. In a large bowl, combine flour, bread crumbs, salt, black pepper and celery salt. Mix well. Whisk eggs in a large bowl. Coat wings with whisked eggs. Dredge wings in seasoned flour/bread crumbs until evenly coated.

2. Melt butter in a large skillet and cook wings over medium heat until golden brown. Set wings aside.

3. Add onion, orange juice, ketchup, brown sugar, soy sauce, ground ginger and garlic salt to skillet. Mix thoroughly. Taste, adjust flavoring. Bring mixture to a boil over medium-high heat.

4. Place oven rack in middle position and preheat oven to 350°. Place cooked wings in a large shallow baking dish. Pour skillet mixture over wings.

5. Bake wings 20 minutes. Remove dish from oven and turn wings. Bake 10 – 20 minutes until done. Baste with dish juices. Internal temperature of wings should be at least 165°.

NOTES: Date: _____

RATE THIS RECIPE
○ ○ ○ ○ ○

ORANGE JUICE / GARLIC WINGS

Marinate | Oven

	INGREDIENTS	SUBSTITUTIONS
☐ 12	wings segmented, tips discarded – rinsed/dried	
☐ 1	cup orange juice	_____
☐ 2	garlic cloves – minced	_____
☐ 1	teaspoon ground ginger	_____
☐ 2	teaspoons Worcestershire sauce	_____
☐ ¼	cup soy sauce	_____
☐ 3	tablespoons brown sugar – packed	_____
☐ ½	teaspoon black pepper	_____

1. In a large bowl, combine all ingredients except wings and mix thoroughly. Taste, adjust flavoring.

2. Place wings in a re-sealable plastic bag. Pour mixture into bag over wings. Seal bag and refrigerate 3 hours. Turn bag occasionally to marinate wings evenly.

3. Place oven rack in middle position and heat oven to 375°. Line a large jelly roll baking pan with aluminum foil and coat with no-stick cooking spray. Arrange wings on pan. Spoon some marinade over wings.

4. Bake 20 minutes. Remove pan from oven, turn wings and baste with pan juices. Bake additional 10 – 20 minutes until done. Internal temperature of wings should be at least 165°.

5. Remove pan from oven, spoon any remaining pan juices over wings, platter and cover with aluminum foil until ready to serve.

NOTES: Date: '7/30/11

RATE THIS RECIPE
○ ○ ○ ◕ ○

ORANGE JUICE / GINGER GLAZED WINGS

Marinate | Oven

	INGREDIENTS	SUBSTITUTIONS
☐	12 wings segmented, tips discarded – rinsed/dried	
☐	½ cup orange juice concentrate – thawed/undiluted	_____
☐	2 tablespoons ground ginger	_____
☐	1 garlic clove – minced	_____
☐	1 teaspoon seasoned salt	_____
☐	4 tablespoons lemon juice	_____
☐	2 tablespoons lime juice	_____
☐	¼ cup hoisin sauce	_____
☐	1 tablespoon extra virgin olive oil	_____
☐	½ cup white sugar	_____

1. Place all ingredients except wings in a large re-sealable plastic bag. Mix well. Taste, adjust flavoring. Add wings to bag and shake to coat wings thoroughly. Seal bag and refrigerate 3 hours.

2. Place oven rack in middle position and preheat oven to 350°. Line a large jelly roll pan with aluminum foil and coat liberally with no-stick cooking spray. Place wings on baking pan and spoon marinade over wings.

3. Bake wings 20 minutes. Remove pan from oven, turn and baste wings with pan juices. Bake additional 10 – 20 minutes until done. Internal temperature of wings should be at least 165°.

NOTES: Date: _____

RATE THIS RECIPE
○ ○ ○ ○ ○

79

ORANGE JUICE / HOISIN GLAZED WINGS
Oven

	INGREDIENTS	SUBSTITUTIONS
☐	12 wings segmented, tips discarded – rinsed/dried	
☐	1 can (6 ounce) frozen orange juice concentrate	_____
☐	3 tablespoons hoisin sauce	_____
☐	½ teaspoon onion powder	_____
☐	2 teaspoons honey	_____
☐	1 tablespoon soy sauce	_____
☐	1 teaspoon cider vinegar	_____
☐	¼ teaspoon red pepper flakes – crushed	_____

1. Place oven rack in middle position and preheat oven to 350°. Line a large jelly roll pan with aluminum foil and coat liberally with no-stick cooking spray.

2. Place wings on baking pan. Bake wings 20 minutes. Remove pan from oven and turn wings. Bake additional 10 – 20 minutes until done. Internal temperature of wings should be at least 165°.

3. Place orange juice concentrate, hoisin sauce, onion powder, honey, soy sauce, vinegar and red pepper flakes in a small saucepan and bring to a simmer over medium-high heat. Taste, adjust flavoring. Simmer until mixture is reduce to ½ cup. Remove from heat and cool. Pour sauce into a large bowl.

4. Plunge wings into bowl and toss to coat completely. Remove wings with a slotted spoon.

NOTES: Date: _____

RATE THIS RECIPE
○ ○ ○ ○ ○

ORANGE MARMALADE / HONEY WINGS

Marinate | Oven

	INGREDIENTS	SUBSTITUTIONS
☐ 12	wings segmented, tips discarded – rinsed/dried	
☐ 1	cup orange marmalade	_____
☐ ½	cup honey	_____
☐ ⅓	cup soy sauce	_____
☐ 2	tablespoons lime juice	_____
☐ 1	tablespoon cider vinegar	_____
☐ 1	tablespoon ground ginger	_____
☐ 2	garlic cloves – minced	_____
☐ ¼	teaspoon red pepper flakes – crushed	_____

1. Whisk all ingredients except wings in a medium bowl and blend together. Taste, adjust flavoring. Place wings in a re-sealable plastic bag. Pour half of mixture into bag. Refrigerate and marinate wings 3 hours turning bag several times. Refrigerate other half of marinade to use as a dipping sauce.

2. Place oven rack in middle position and preheat oven to 350°. Line a large jelly roll baking pan with aluminum foil and coat liberally with no-stick cooking spray. Place wings on pan. Spoon bag marinade over wings.

3. Bake wings 20 minutes. Remove pan from oven, turn wings and baste with pan juices. Bake additional 10 – 20 minutes until done. Internal temperature of wings should be at least 165°.

4. Remove pan from oven, platter wings and cover with aluminum foil until ready to serve. Use saved marinade as a dipping sauce.

NOTES: Date: _____

RATE THIS RECIPE
○ ○ ○ ○ ○

ORANGE MARMALADE / KETCHUP WINGS

Marinate | Oven

INGREDIENTS	SUBSTITUTIONS
☐ 12 wings segmented, tips discarded – rinsed/dried	
☐ 1 jar (10 ounce) orange marmalade	_____
☐ ½ cup ketchup	_____
☐ 2 tablespoons chili powder	_____
☐ 1½ tablespoons cider vinegar	_____
☐ ¾ stick butter	_____
☐ ½ cup brown sugar – packed	_____
☐ 1 tablespoon onion – dried minced	_____
☐ 1 tablespoon ground ginger	_____
☐ 1 tablespoon Worcestershire sauce	_____
☐ 1 tablespoon hot pepper sauce	_____

1. In a large saucepan, combine all ingredients except wings and mix well. Taste, adjust flavorings. Bring to a boil. Reduce heat and simmer uncovered 10 minutes. Cool.

2. Place wings in a large re-sealable plastic bag. Pour mixture over wings. Seal bag and refrigerate 3 hours.

3. Place oven rack in middle position and heat oven to 375°. Line a large jelly roll pan with aluminum foil and coat with a no-stick cooking spray. Transfer wings to pan. Spoon some marinade over wings. Discard bag and remaining marinade.

4. Bake wings 20 minutes. Remove pan from oven, turn wings and baste with pan juices. Bake additional 10 – 20 minutes until done. Internal temperature of wings should be at least 165°.

NOTES: Date: _____

RATE THIS RECIPE
○ ○ ○ ○ ○

PEACH CHUTNEY / DRY ONION SOUP WINGS
Oven

		INGREDIENTS	SUBSTITUTIONS
☐	12	wings segmented, tips discarded – rinsed/dried	
☐	1	cup peach chutney	_____
☐	1	package (1.25 ounce) dry onion soup mix	_____
☐	½	teaspoon garlic powder	_____
☐	¾	cup mayonnaise	_____
☐	½	cup hot water	_____
☐	⅛	teaspoon salt	_____
☐	½	teaspoon black pepper	_____

1. In a medium bowl, stir together peach chutney, onion soup mix, garlic powder, mayonnaise and hot water. Mix well. Taste, adjust flavoring.

2. Place wings in a large baking dish. Spoon two-thirds of mixture over wings. Season wings with salt and black pepper.

3. Place oven rack in middle position and preheat oven to 350°. Bake 20 minutes. Remove dish from oven, turn wings and spoon remaining third of mixture over wings. Return to oven and bake additional 10 – 20 minutes until done. Internal temperature of wings should be at least 165°.

4. Remove wings with a slotted spoon. Platter wings and cover with aluminum foil until ready to serve.

NOTES: Date: _____

RATE THIS RECIPE
○ ○ ○ ○ ○

PINEAPPLE BARBECUED WINGS

Oven

		INGREDIENTS	SUBSTITUTIONS
☐	12	wings segmented, tips discarded – rinsed/dried	
☐	2	cans (8 ounce) pineapple tidbits	_____
☐	½	cup barbecue sauce	_____
☐	2	tablespoons picante sauce	_____
☐	1	tablespoon cider vinegar	_____
☐	½	tablespoon soy sauce	_____
☐	¼	teaspoon black pepper	_____
☐	¼	teaspoon salt	_____

1. Save ¼ cup of pineapple juice from tidbits and discard rest of juice. Mix together pineapple, barbecue sauce, picante sauce, vinegar and soy sauce. Add pineapple juice to mixture. Mix thoroughly. Taste, adjust flavorings.

2. Place wings in a large shallow baking dish. Season wings with salt and black pepper. Spoon half of pineapple mixture equally over wings.

3. Place oven rack in middle position. Preheat oven to 350°. Bake 20 minutes. Remove wings from oven, turn and baste with remaining mixture. Bake additional 10 – 20 minutes until wings are done. Internal temperature of wings should be at least 165°.

4. Remove wings with a slotted spoon, place on a platter and spoon any remaining sauce from pan over wings. Cover with aluminum foil until ready to serve.

NOTES: Date: _____

Most fires are the result of unattended cooking. Keep a sharp eye on pots and pans, both on the stove top and in the oven.

Always, *always* have a properly rated fire extinguisher within arms reach. Familiarize yourself with the instructions and practice a dry-run so you can operate it if and when needed.

Never, *never* attempt to put out a grease fire with water. You will only cause the oil to erupt and this will spread the fire around the kitchen, and, in all probability, throughout the house.

PINEAPPLE JUICE / BUTTER BREADED WINGS
Oven

		INGREDIENTS	SUBSTITUTIONS
☐	12	wings segmented, tips discarded – rinsed/dried	
☐	½	cup all-purpose flour	_____
☐	½	cup bread crumbs	_____
☐	¼	teaspoon garlic salt	_____
☐	½	teaspoon lemon pepper seasoning	_____
☐	2	eggs – beaten	_____
☐	¾	stick butter	_____
☐	¾	cup white sugar	_____
☐	½	cup cider vinegar	_____
☐	¼	cup pineapple juice	_____
☐	¼	cup ketchup	_____
☐	1	teaspoon soy sauce	_____

1.   Place flour, bread crumbs, garlic salt and lemon pepper in a large re-sealable plastic bag. Whisk eggs in a bowl until smooth. Moisten wings in egg bowl. Place wings in bag, seal and toss to coat thoroughly.

2.   Heat butter in a large skillet and cook wings on each side until golden brown.

3.   Place oven rack in middle position and preheat oven to 375°. Line a large jelly roll pan with aluminum foil and coat with a no-stick cooking spray. Remove wings from skillet and arrange wings on baking pan.

4.   In a medium saucepan, combine white sugar, vinegar, pineapple juice, ketchup and soy sauce. Taste, adjust flavoring. Bring to a boil and blend thoroughly. Spoon mixture over wings.

5.   Bake in oven 20 minutes. Remove pan from oven, turn wings and baste with pan juices. Bake additional 10 – 20 minutes until done. Internal temperature of wings should be least 165°.

NOTES: Date: _____

RATE THIS RECIPE
○ ○ ○ ○ ○

PINEAPPLE JUICE / HABAÑERO WINGS

Marinate | Grill

INGREDIENTS	SUBSTITUTIONS
☐ 12 wings segmented, tips discarded – rinsed/dried	
☐ 1 cup pineapple juice	_____
☐ 2 habañero chiles – finely chopped	_____
☐ ¼ teaspoon salt	_____
☐ ¼ teaspoon black pepper	_____
☐ ½ teaspoon ground allspice	_____
☐ 2 tablespoons balsamic vinegar	_____
☐ 2 tablespoons brown sugar	_____
☐ 4 garlic cloves – finely chopped	_____

1. Combine all ingredients except wings in a saucepan and bring to a boil. Boil 2 minutes. Taste, adjust flavoring. Remove from heat and cool to room temperature.

2. Pour mixture into a large re-sealable plastic bag. Add wings to bag and marinate in refrigerator 3 hours.

3. Spray grill grates with no-stick cooking spray. Prepare grill to a medium high-direct heat. Grill 10 – 15 minutes until done. Internal temperature should be at least 165º. Serve with blue cheese dip. See blue cheese dip recipes in appendix.

NOTES: Date: _____

RATE THIS RECIPE
○ ○ ○ ○ ○

PINEAPPLE JUICE WINGS

Marinate | Oven

		INGREDIENTS	SUBSTITUTIONS
☐	12	wings segmented, tips discarded – rinsed/dried	
☐	½	cup pineapple juice – unsweetened	_____
☐	¼	cup soy sauce	_____
☐	¼	cup vegetable oil	_____
☐	½	cup white sugar	_____
☐	½	cup water	_____
☐	1	teaspoon garlic powder	_____
☐	½	teaspoon ground ginger	_____

1. Combine pineapple juice, soy sauce, vegetable oil, white sugar, water, garlic powder and ginger in a large re-sealable plastic bag and mix thoroughly. Taste, adjust flavoring. Add wings and toss to coat thoroughly. Seal bag and refrigerate 3 hours.

2. Place oven rack in middle position. Preheat oven to 350°. Cover baking sheet with aluminum foil. Spray foil with no-stick cooking spray. Place wings on baking sheet. Bake 35 – 45 minutes until done. Internal temperature of wings should be at least 165°.

NOTES:

Date: _____

RATE THIS RECIPE
○ ○ ○ ○ ○

PLUM / JALAPEÑO GRILLED WINGS

Grill

INGREDIENTS	SUBSTITUTIONS
☐ 12 wings segmented, tips discarded – rinsed/dried	
☐ 5 plums – skinned/pitted/coarsely chopped	_____
☐ ½ can (7 ounce) pickled jalapeño peppers with juice	_____
☐ 2 tablespoons duck sauce	_____
☐ 1 tablespoon corn syrup	_____
☐ 3 teaspoons Dijon mustard	_____
☐ ¼ teaspoon Worcestershire sauce	_____
☐ ¼ teaspoon salt	_____
☐ ¼ teaspoon black pepper	_____

1. Place plums, peppers/juice, duck sauce, syrup, Dijon mustard, Worcestershire, salt and black pepper in a blender and purée. Reserve a quarter of sauce to serve with wings.

2. Spray grill grates with no-stick cooking spray. Prepare grill to medium-direct heat. Place wings directly over heat and baste with sauce. Grill wings on each side until done. Baste frequently with sauce. Turn wings frequently to avoid burning. Internal temperature of wings should be at least 165°.

3. Transfer wings from grill to a platter. Spoon reserved sauce over wings. Serve with blue cheese dip. See blue cheese dip recipes in appendix.

NOTES: Date: _____

RATE THIS RECIPE
○ ○ ○ ○ ○

PLUM JAM / HORSERADISH WINGS

Oven

✔

INGREDIENTS	SUBSTITUTIONS
☐ 12 wings segmented, tips discarded – rinsed/dried	
☐ ½ cup plum jam	_____
☐ 2 tablespoons prepared horseradish	_____
☐ 1 tablespoon Dijon mustard	_____
☐ 3 tablespoons soy sauce	_____
☐ 1 teaspoon hot pepper sauce	_____

1. Place all ingredients except wings in a bowl. Mix thoroughly. Taste, adjust flavoring.

2. Place oven rack in middle position. Preheat oven to 350º. Cover baking sheet with aluminum foil. Spray foil with no-stick cooking spray. Place wings on foil.

3. Brush wings liberally with plum mixture. Bake wings 35 – 45 minutes until done. Turn several times and baste with plum mixture. Internal temperature of wings should be at least 165º. Serve with blue cheese dip. See blue cheese dip recipes in appendix.

NOTES: Date: _____

RATE THIS RECIPE
○ ○ ○ ○ ○

RAISIN / COCONUT WINGS
Stove Top

INGREDIENTS	SUBSTITUTIONS
☐ 12 wings segmented, tips discarded – rinsed/dried	
☐ ½ cup dark raisins	_____
☐ 1 cup coconut milk – unsweetened	_____
☐ 1 tomato – seeded/chopped	_____
☐ 2 teaspoons cilantro – dried chopped	_____
☐ 1 tablespoon curry powder	_____
☐ 1 tablespoon hot pepper sauce	_____
☐ 1½ tablespoons soy sauce	_____
☐ ½ tablespoon nutmeg	_____
☐ 1 teaspoon orange zest	_____
☐ 3 tablespoons extra virgin olive oil	_____
☐ 1 tablespoon ground ginger	_____
☐ 1 garlic clove – minced	_____

1. In a bowl, combine raisins, coconut milk, tomato, cilantro, curry powder, hot pepper sauce, soy sauce, nutmeg and orange zest. Mix thoroughly. Taste, adjust flavoring.

2. In a large deep skillet, heat oil and sauté ginger and garlic 1 minute. Add coconut milk mixture. Bring to a boil and reduce heat. Add wings to skillet. Cover and simmer until most of sauce evaporates and forms a glaze on wings and wings are done, 40 – 50 minutes. Stir occasionally. Internal temperature of wings should be at least 165°.

3. Remove wings from skillet, platter wings and cover with aluminum foil until ready to serve.

NOTES: Date: _____

RATE THIS RECIPE
○ ○ ○ ○ ○

RASPBERRY JAM WINGS

Oven

		INGREDIENTS	SUBSTITUTIONS
☐	12	wings segmented, tips discarded – rinsed/dried	
☐	1	cup raspberry jam – seedless	_____
☐	⅔	cup barbecue sauce	_____
☐	3	green onions – finely chopped	_____
☐	1	garlic clove – minced	_____
☐	1	teaspoon horseradish	_____
☐	¼	teaspoon liquid smoke	_____
☐	¼	teaspoon salt	_____
☐	1	onion – thinly sliced	_____
☐	1	tablespoon garlic salt	_____

1. In a bowl, combine raspberry jam, barbecue sauce, onion, garlic, horseradish, liquid smoke and salt and mix well. Taste, adjust flavoring.

2. Place oven rack in middle position and preheat oven to 350°. Line a large jelly roll baking pan with aluminum foil and coat with no-stick cooking spray. Place wings on pan. Spoon raspberry mixture over wings. Spread sliced onion over wings. Sprinkle garlic salt over wings and onions.

3. Bake wings 20 minutes. Remove pan from oven. Spoon drippings from bottom of pan over wings and onions without disturbing onions. Bake additional 10 – 20 minutes until done. Internal temperature of wings should be at least 165°.

4. Remove pan from oven, platter wings and cover with aluminum foil until ready to serve.

NOTES: Date: _____

RATE THIS RECIPE
○ ○ ○ ○ ○

RASPBERRY JAM GLAZED WINGS

Marinate | Oven

		INGREDIENTS	SUBSTITUTIONS
☐	12	wings segmented, tips discarded – rinsed/dried	
☐	1	cup raspberry jam – seedless	_____
☐	¼	cup soy sauce	_____
☐	¼	cup cider vinegar	_____
☐	1	garlic clove – minced	_____
☐	1	teaspoon ground ginger	_____
☐	½	teaspoon onion salt	_____
☐	1	teaspoon black pepper	_____

1. In a large saucepan, combine raspberry jam, soy sauce, vinegar, garlic, ginger, onion salt and black pepper. Bring to a boil, reduce heat and simmer 2 minutes. Taste, adjust flavorings. Cool mixture.

2. Place wings in a large re-sealable plastic bag. Pour half of mixture over wings. Seal bag and refrigerate 3 hours. Pour rest of marinade in a bowl, cover and set aside in refrigerator. Marinade is to be reduced for basting.

3. Place oven rack in middle position and preheat oven to 350°. Line a large jelly roll baking pan with aluminum foil. Coat foil with a no-stick cooking spray. Place wings on baking pan. Bake wings 20 minutes.

4. Meanwhile, place set aside raspberry mixture in a saucepan and bring to a boil. Reduce heat and simmer until sauce thickens, about 10 minutes.

5. Remove wings from oven and baste with reduced mixture. Bake additional 10 – 20 minutes until done. Internal temperature of wings should be at least 165°.

NOTES: Date: _____

RATE THIS RECIPE
○ ○ ○ ○ ○

VEGETABLE AND NUT WINGS

CHILI SAUCE / ONION / MOLASSES WINGS
Slow Cooker

INGREDIENTS	SUBSTITUTIONS
☐ 12 wings segmented, tips discarded – rinsed/dried	
☐ ½ cup chili sauce	_____
☐ ¼ cup molasses	_____
☐ ½ teaspoon hot pepper sauce	_____
☐ ½ tablespoon chili powder	_____
☐ ¼ cup lemon juice	_____
☐ 1 tablespoon Worcestershire sauce	_____
☐ 1 onion – chopped	_____
☐ 2 garlic cloves – minced	_____
☐ 1 tablespoon salsa	_____
☐ ½ teaspoon salt	_____

1. Combine all ingredients except wings in a slow cooker and mix thoroughly. Taste, adjust flavoring.

2. Add wings to slow cooker and coat thoroughly. Cook wings on low 3 – 4 hours until done. Turn wings once during cooking. Internal temperature of wings should be at least 165°. Resist removing lid too often. Slow cooking requires internal heat and condensation.

3. Remove wings with a slotted spoon.

NOTES: Date: _____

RATE THIS RECIPE
○ ○ ○ ○ ○

GINGER / GARLIC WINGS
Oven

	INGREDIENTS	SUBSTITUTIONS
☐	12 wings segmented, tips discarded – rinsed/dried	
☐	4 garlic cloves – finely minced	_____
☐	3 tablespoons ginger – finely grated	_____
☐	¼ teaspoon cayenne pepper	_____
☐	½ cup cider vinegar	_____
☐	½ cup brown sugar – packed	_____
☐	1 teaspoon soy sauce	_____

1. Place all ingredients except wings in a saucepan and bring to a boil 2 minutes over medium heat. Taste, adjust flavoring. Set aside in a large bowl.

2. Place oven rack in middle position. Preheat oven to 350°. Cover baking sheet with aluminum foil. Spray foil with no-stick cooking spray. Place wings on baking sheet and bake 35 – 45 minutes until done. Internal temperature of wings should be at least 165°. Plunge wings into set aside sauce and toss to coat thoroughly. Serve with blue cheese dip. See recipes in appendix.

NOTES: Date: _____

RATE THIS RECIPE
○ ○ ○ ○ ○

HERB / FENNEL WINGS

Grill

INGREDIENTS	SUBSTITUTIONS
☐ 12 wings segmented, tips discarded – rinsed/dried	
☐ 2 tablespoons fennel – crushed	_____
☐ 1½ tablespoons Herbes de Provence	_____
☐ 2 tablespoons extra virgin olive oil	_____
☐ 1 tablespoon cumin	_____

1. Add fennel, Herbes de Provence, oil and cumin in a bowl. Mix thoroughly.

2. Massage rub thoroughly over all parts of wings.

3. Spray grill grates with a no-stick cooking spray. Prepare grill to medium direct heat. Grill wings 8 – 10 minutes on each side until done. Turn wings frequently to avoid burning. Internal temperature of wings should be at least 165°.

4. Transfer wings from grill to a platter.

NOTES:

Date: _____

RATE THIS RECIPE
○ ○ ○ ○ ○

HERBES DE PROVENCE / ALLSPICE WINGS
Stove Top | Oven

INGREDIENTS		SUBSTITUTIONS
☐ 12	wings segmented, tips discarded – rinsed/dried	
☐ 1	small onion – minced	_____
☐ 1½	tablespoons Herbes de Provence	_____
☐ 1½	teaspoons ground allspice	_____
☐ 2	garlic cloves – minced	_____
☐ ¼	cup soy sauce	_____
☐ ½	teaspoon ground cinnamon	_____
☐ ½	teaspoon ground cloves	_____
☐ ½	teaspoon onion powder	_____
☐ ½	teaspoon ground ginger	_____

1. Place wings and minced onion in a stockpot and fill with enough water to cover wings. Bring stockpot to a boil, reduce heat and simmer wings 20 minutes.

2. Combine all other ingredients in a saucepan and warm over medium heat. Taste, adjust flavoring.

3. Drain water from wings and replace with soy sauce mixture. Coat all wings thoroughly.

4. Place oven rack in middle position and preheat oven to 350°. Line a large jelly roll pan with aluminum foil and coat liberally with no-stick cooking spray. Place wings on pan. Spoon some of mixture over wings.

5. Bake wings 25 – 35 minutes in oven until done. Internal temperature of wings should be at least 165°.

NOTES: Date: _____

RATE THIS RECIPE
○ ○ ○ ○ ○

JALAPEÑO / HORSERADISH WINGS
Marinate | Deep Fry

		INGREDIENTS	SUBSTITUTIONS
☐	12	wings segmented, tips discarded – rinsed/dried	
☐	2	jalapeño peppers – roughly chopped	_____
☐	1	tablespoon prepared horseradish	_____
☐	¼	cup extra virgin olive oil	_____
☐	1	teaspoon mustard powder	_____
☐	2	teaspoons wasabi paste	_____
☐	1	tablespoon cider vinegar	_____
☐	1	teaspoon white sugar	_____
☐	1	teaspoon salt	_____
☐		canola oil or peanut oil for deep frying	_____

1. Purée all ingredients except wings in a food processor. Taste, adjust flavoring. Place puréed ingredients into a large re-sealable plastic bag. Add wings and toss to coat thoroughly. Refrigerate and marinate 3 hours.

2. Place enough oil in a heavy skillet or deep fryer to cover wings. Heat oil to 375º. Shake off excess coating on wings and add to oil and cook until done. Internal temperature of wings should be at least 165º. Drain wings on paper towels. Serve with blue cheese dip. See blue cheese dip recipes in appendix.

NOTES: Date: _____

RATE THIS RECIPE
○ ○ ○ ○ ○

ONION CRISP WINGS
Oven

	INGREDIENTS	SUBSTITUTIONS
☐ 12	wings segmented, tips discarded – rinsed/dried	
☐ 2	cups potato chips – crushed fine	_____
☐ 1	can (2.8 ounce) French fried onions – crushed fine	_____
☐ ½	cup dry bread crumbs	_____
☐ 1	teaspoon dried oregano	_____
☐ 1	teaspoon onion salt	_____
☐ ½	teaspoon garlic powder	_____
☐ 1	teaspoon paprika	_____
☐ 2	eggs – beaten	_____
☐ 2	tablespoons milk	_____
☐ ½	stick butter	_____

1. Crush potato chips and French fried onions into minute pieces. Combine potato chips and French fried onions in a large re–sealable plastic bag. Add bread crumbs, oregano, onion salt, garlic powder and paprika to plastic bag. Mix well.

2. Whisk milk and eggs in a bowl until blended. Dip wings in egg mixture. Place wings in bag and shake to coat wings evenly.

3. Melt butter in a small saucepan.

4. Place oven rack in middle position. Preheat oven to 350°. Line a large jelly roll baking pan with aluminum foil and coat liberally with no-stick cooking spray.

5. Place wings on prepared pan. Dab or spoon butter evenly over wings. Bake wings 20 minutes. Turn, baste with pan juices and bake additional 10 – 20 minutes until done. Internal temperature of wings should be at least 165°.

6. Serve with blue cheese dip. See blue cheese dip recipes in appendix.

NOTES: Date: _____

RATE THIS RECIPE

○ ○ ○ ○ ○

ONION / HONEY WINGS

Slow Cooker

		INGREDIENTS	SUBSTITUTIONS
☐	12	wings segmented, tips discarded – rinsed/dried	
☐	1	onion – chopped	_____
☐	3	tablespoons honey	_____
☐	¼	cup soy sauce	_____
☐	1	tablespoon ground ginger	_____
☐	2	garlic cloves – minced	_____
☐	2	tablespoons molasses	_____
☐	1	tablespoon paprika	_____
☐	2	tablespoons extra virgin olive oil	_____

1. Combine all ingredients except wings in a slow cooker. Mix thoroughly. Taste, adjust flavoring.

2. Add wings to slow cooker and coat thoroughly. Cover and cook on low 3 – 5 hours until done. Turn wings halfway through cooking. Internal temperature of wings should be at least 165°. Resist removing lid too often. Slow cooking requires internal heat and condensation for cooking.

3. Remove wings with a slotted spoon. Platter wings and cover with aluminum foil until ready to serve.

NOTES: Date: _____

RATE THIS RECIPE
○ ○ ○ ○ ○

ONION / ALLSPICE WINGS
Marinate | Oven

		INGREDIENTS	SUBSTITUTIONS
☐	12	wings segmented, tips discarded – rinsed/dried	
☐	1	onion – chopped	_____
☐	3	scallions – white only/finely chopped	_____
☐	2	garlic cloves – minced	_____
☐	½	teaspoon dried thyme	_____
☐	1	teaspoon salt	_____
☐	1½	teaspoons ground allspice	_____
☐	½	teaspoon paprika	_____
☐	¼	teaspoon ground nutmeg	_____
☐	½	teaspoon cinnamon	_____
☐	1	teaspoon black pepper	_____
☐	½	teaspoon hot pepper sauce	_____
☐	2	tablespoons soy sauce	_____
☐	¼	cup extra virgin olive oil	_____

1. In a blender, purée all ingredients except wings. Taste, adjust flavoring. Place wings in a large re-sealable plastic bag. Pour mixture into bag, seal and refrigerate 3 hours. Turn bag occasionally to coat wings thoroughly.

2. Place oven rack in middle position and preheat oven to 350°. Line a large jelly roll pan with aluminum foil and coat liberally with no-stick cooking spray. Place wings on pan. Spoon some marinade over wings. Discard bag and remaining marinade.

3. Bake wings 35 – 45 minutes in oven until done. Internal temperature of wings should be at least 165°.

NOTES: Date: _____

RATE THIS RECIPE
○ ○ ○ ○ ○

ONION / TOMATO PASTE WINGS

Slow Cooker

		INGREDIENTS	SUBSTITUTIONS
☐	12	wings segmented, tips discarded – rinsed/dried	
☐	2	large onions – chopped	_____
☐	2	cans (6 ounce) tomato paste	_____
☐	1	garlic clove – minced	_____
☐	¼	cup Worcestershire sauce	_____
☐	2	teaspoons soy sauce	_____
☐	¼	cup cider vinegar	_____
☐	½	cup brown sugar – packed	_____
☐	½	cup sweet pickle relish	_____
☐	½	cup red wine	_____
☐	1	teaspoon salt	_____
☐	2	teaspoons dry mustard	_____

1. Combine all ingredients except wings in slow cooker and blend thoroughly. Taste, adjust flavoring.

2. Place wings in slow cooker and coat thoroughly. Cook on low 3 – 5 hours until done. Turn wings once during cooking process. Internal temperature of wings should be at least 165°. Resist removing lid too often. Slow cooking requires internal heat and condensation for cooking.

3. Remove wings with a slotted spoon. Platter wings and cover with aluminum foil until ready to serve.

NOTES: Date: _____

RATE THIS RECIPE
○ ○ ○ ○ ○

PEANUT BUTTER / BEER WINGS

Oven

INGREDIENTS	SUBSTITUTIONS
☐ 12 wings segmented, tips discarded – rinsed/dried	
☐ ¼ cup creamy peanut butter	_____
☐ 1 cup beer	_____
☐ 1½ tablespoons chili powder	_____
☐ ¼ cup lime juice	_____
☐ ½ teaspoon dry mustard	_____
☐ ¼ cup dark molasses	_____
☐ ¼ cup Worcestershire sauce	_____
☐ ¼ teaspoon anise seed – toasted	_____
☐ ¼ teaspoon salt	_____

1. Combine all ingredients except wings in a large heavy pan. Simmer over medium heat 15 – 20 minutes until reduced and thickened. Taste, adjust flavoring.

2. Add wings to sauce and toss to coat.

3. Place oven rack in middle position. Preheat oven to 350º. Spread wings over a large, rimmed baking sheet and cover with sauce. Bake 20 minutes. Turn wings. Cook 10 – 20 minutes until done. Internal temperature of wings should be at least 165º. Serve with blue cheese dip. See blue cheese dip recipes in appendix.

NOTES:

Date: _____

RATE THIS RECIPE
○ ○ ○ ○ ○

PEANUT BUTTER DIP WINGS

Oven

INGREDIENTS		SUBSTITUTIONS
☐	12 wings segmented, tips discarded – rinsed/dried	
☐	¾ cup teriyaki sauce	_____
☐	2 tablespoons hoisin sauce	_____
☐	¼ cup soy sauce	_____
☐	1 garlic clove – minced	_____
☐	⅓ cup creamy peanut butter	_____
☐	1 tablespoon cider vinegar	_____

1. In a large bowl, mix together teriyaki sauce and hoisin sauce. Add wings and toss until wings are evenly coated.

2. Put soy sauce, garlic, peanut butter and vinegar in blender. Blend until smooth. Taste, adjust flavoring. Pour mixture into a large bowl. Set aside.

3. Place oven rack in middle position and preheat oven to 350°. Line a large jelly roll baking pan with aluminum foil and coat with no-stick cooking spray.

4. Place wings on pan and bake 20 minutes. Remove pan from oven, turn wings and baste with pan juices. Bake additional 10 – 20 minutes until done. Internal temperature of wings should be at least 165°.

5. Plunge wings into peanut butter mixture and coat wings. Platter wings and cover with aluminum foil until ready to serve.

NOTES:

Date: _____

RATE THIS RECIPE
○ ○ ○ ○ ○

PEANUT BUTTER / HONEY WINGS
Marinate | Oven

	INGREDIENTS	SUBSTITUTIONS
☐	12 wings segmented, tips discarded – rinsed/dried	
☐	½ cup creamy peanut butter	_____
☐	½ cup honey	_____
☐	2 tablespoons soy sauce	_____
☐	3 tablespoons peanut oil	_____
☐	1 garlic clove – minced	_____
☐	1 teaspoon ground ginger	_____
☐	1 teaspoon allspice	_____
☐	1 teaspoon curry powder	_____

1. In a large mixing bowl, mix all ingredients except wings until well blended. Taste, adjust flavorings. Place wings in a re-sealable plastic bag. Pour sauce over wings, seal bag and marinate 3 hours in refrigerator. Turn bag several times while marinating.

2. Place oven rack in middle position and preheat oven to 350°. Transfer wings and sauce to a large shallow baking dish. Spoon some sauce over wings.

3. Bake wings 20 minutes. Remove dish from oven, turn wings and baste with pan juices. Bake additional 10 – 20 minutes until done. Internal temperature of wings should be at least 165°.

4. Remove dish from oven, platter wings and cover with aluminum foil until ready to serve.

NOTES:

Date: _____

RATE THIS RECIPE
○ ○ ○ ○ ○

PEANUT BUTTER SAUCE WINGS

Oven

		INGREDIENTS	SUBSTITUTIONS
☐	12	wings segmented, tips discarded – rinsed/dried	
☐	3	tablespoons peanut oil	_____
☐	2	tablespoons ground ginger	_____
☐	1	garlic clove – minced	_____
☐	3	tablespoons creamy peanut butter	_____
☐	1	tablespoon lime juice	_____
☐	½	teaspoon cayenne pepper	_____
☐	2	teaspoons soy sauce	_____
☐	1	tablespoon white sugar	_____
☐	½	teaspoon red pepper flakes – crushed	_____

1. Place oil, ginger and garlic in a large bowl and mix thoroughly. Add wings and coat thoroughly.

2. Place oven rack in middle position and preheat oven to 350°. Line a large jelly roll baking pan with aluminum foil and coat with no-stick cooking spray.

3. Place wings on pan and bake 20 minutes. Turn wings and bake additional 10 – 20 minutes until done. Internal temperature of wings should be at least 165°.

4. Meanwhile, combine peanut butter, lime juice, cayenne pepper, soy sauce, white sugar and red pepper flakes in a large bowl and blend until smooth. Taste, adjust flavoring.

5. Plunge wings into peanut butter sauce and coat thoroughly. Remove wings with a slotted spoon. Platter wings and cover with aluminum foil until ready to serve.

NOTES: Date: _____

RATE THIS RECIPE
○ ○ ○ ○ ○

Take recommendations about operating a safe kitchen seriously. During one particularly memorable visit with my son's family, I was using their open flame gas stove to cook for my grandchildren. I was wearing a robe with a fine nap, and as I was sautéing onions in a skillet, flames shot up the sleeve! I got the robe off quickly, bunched it in a pile on the floor and smothered the flames. I was lucky I wasn't seriously injured. Instead, I was just a bit chilly.

Also, I burned myself more than a couple of times by grabbing the handle of my cast-iron skillet after it had been in a hot oven. I learned, rather slowly, to make oven mitts my constant cooking companions. Learn from my mistakes and use those oven mitts! Stay safe. Nothing ruins a cooking adventure faster than a fire, a cut or a burn.

PEANUTS / BACON WINGS
Marinate | Oven

	INGREDIENTS	SUBSTITUTIONS
☐	12 wings segmented, tips discarded – rinsed/dried	
☐	½ cup soy sauce	_____
☐	⅓ cup dry sherry	_____
☐	3 tablespoons brown sugar – packed	_____
☐	3 tablespoons honey	_____
☐	2 tablespoons hoisin sauce	_____
☐	2 tablespoons teriyaki sauce	_____
☐	1 garlic clove – minced	_____
☐	½ teaspoon black pepper	_____
☐	12 bacon slices	_____
☐	½ cup unsalted peanuts – finely crushed	_____

1. In a medium bowl, mix soy sauce, sherry, brown sugar, honey, hoisin sauce, teriyaki sauce, garlic and pepper. Taste, adjust flavoring. Place wings in a re-sealable plastic bag. Pour sauce over wings, seal bag and marinate 3 hours in refrigerator. Turn bag several times while marinating.

2. Cut bacon slices in half. Marinate bacon with wings the last 20 minutes of marinating. Retrieve bacon and set aside.

3. Place finely crushed peanuts in a second re-sealable plastic bag. Add wings and coat with peanuts. Wrap wings loosely with bacon. (Bacon will shrink while cooking. Use a portion of a toothpick to secure and pin bacon to wing.)

4. Place oven rack in middle position and preheat oven to 350°. Line large jelly roll baking pan with aluminum foil and coat with no-stick cooking spray. Place wings on pan. Brush marinade over wings.

5. Bake wings 20 minutes. Remove pan from oven and turn wings being careful not to disturb bacon. Spoon pan juices over wings. Bake additional 10 – 20 minutes until done. Internal temperature of wings should be at least 165°.

6. Remove pan from oven, platter wings and cover with aluminum foil until ready to serve.

NOTES: Date: _____

RATE THIS RECIPE
○ ○ ○ ○ ○

SCALLIONS / JALAPEÑO HOT SAUCE WINGS

Marinate | Oven

		INGREDIENTS	SUBSTITUTIONS
☐	12	wings segmented, tips discarded – rinsed/dried	
☐	5	scallions – white only/chopped	_____
☐	2	bay leaves	_____
☐	3	tablespoons extra virgin olive oil	_____
☐	1	teaspoon hot pepper sauce	_____
☐	1	garlic clove – minced	_____
☐	1	tablespoon ground ginger	_____
☐	¼	cup green jalapeño hot pepper sauce	_____
☐	1	tablespoon ground allspice	_____
☐	1	tablespoon steak sauce	_____
☐	2½	teaspoons dried thyme	_____
☐	½	teaspoon salt	_____
☐	½	teaspoon black pepper	_____

1. Place all ingredients except wings in a blender and process until a thick paste forms. Pour into a large re-sealable plastic bag and mix well. Add wings , seal bag and toss to coat thoroughly. Refrigerate 3 hours.

2. Place oven rack in middle position and preheat oven to 350°. Line a large jelly roll baking pan with aluminum foil and coat foil with a no-stick cooking spray. Place wings on pan. Spoon some marinade over wings.

3. Bake wings 20 minutes. Remove pan from oven, turn wings and baste with pan juices. Bake additional 10 – 20 minutes until done. Internal temperature of wings should be at least 165°.

NOTES: Date: _____

RATE THIS RECIPE
○ ○ ○ ○ ○

SCALLION ROASTED WINGS

Marinate I Oven

		INGREDIENTS	SUBSTITUTIONS
☐	12	wings segmented, tips discarded – rinsed/dried	
☐	12	scallions – whites only/finely diced	_____
☐	⅓	cup soy sauce	_____
☐	¾	cup rice wine	_____
☐	½	cup water	_____
☐	2	garlic cloves – minced	_____
☐	¼	teaspoon onion powder	_____
☐	¾	teaspoon ground ginger	_____

1. Combine all ingredients except wings in a saucepan and bring to a boil. Reduce heat and simmer mixture 10 minutes. Taste, adjust flavoring. Cool.

2. Place wings in a re-sealable plastic bag and pour three-quarters marinade into bag. Seal bag and marinate 3 hours in refrigerator. Turn bag several times to coat wings thoroughly. Set aside and refrigerate other quarter of marinade.

3. Place oven rack in middle position and preheat oven to 350°. Line a large jelly roll baking pan with aluminum foil and coat liberally with no-stick cooking spray. Place wings on pan and spoon some marinade from bag over wings.

4. Bake 20 minutes. Remove pan from oven, turn wings and baste with remaining quarter of marinade. Bake additional 10 – 20 minutes until done. Internal temperature of wings should be at least 165°.

5. Remove pan from oven, platter wings and cover with aluminum foil until ready to serve.

NOTES: Date: _____

RATE THIS RECIPE
○ ○ ○ ○ ○

HONEY
WINGS

CHILI SAUCE / HONEY WINGS

Oven

		INGREDIENTS	SUBSTITUTIONS
☐	12	wings segmented, tips discarded – rinsed/dried	
☐	¼	cup chili sauce	_____
☐	¼	cup honey	_____
☐	1	tablespoon dried minced onion	_____
☐	1	tablespoon soy sauce	_____
☐	½	teaspoon paprika	_____
☐	½	teaspoon dry mustard	_____
☐	½	teaspoon cayenne pepper	_____
☐	½	teaspoon black pepper	_____

1. Place all ingredients except wings in a bowl and mix thoroughly. Taste, adjust flavoring.

2. Place oven rack in middle position and heat oven to 350°. Line a large jelly roll baking pan with aluminum foil and coat liberally with no-stick cooking spray. Place wings on pan. Spoon mixture over wings and coat wings completely.

3. Bake 20 minutes. Remove pan from oven, turn wings and baste with pan juices. Bake additional 10 – 20 minutes until done. Internal temperature of wings should be at least 165°.

4. Remove pan from oven, platter wings and cover with aluminum foil until ready to serve. Serve wings with any remaining sauce from pan.

NOTES: Date: _____

RATE THIS RECIPE
○ ○ ○ ○ ○

CINNAMON / HONEY GRILLED WINGS
Marinate | Grill

	INGREDIENTS	SUBSTITUTIONS
☐	12 wings segmented, tips discarded – rinsed/dried	
☐	2 teaspoons ground cinnamon	_____
☐	½ cup honey	_____
☐	1 garlic clove – minced	_____
☐	¼ cup extra virgin olive oil	_____
☐	¼ cup cider vinegar	_____
☐	2 tablespoons soy sauce	_____
☐	1 teaspoon paprika	_____
☐	½ teaspoon ground ginger	_____
☐	½ teaspoon dry mustard	_____

1. Combine all ingredients except wings in a bowl and mix thoroughly. Taste, adjust flavoring. Reserve a quarter of mixture in a bowl, cover and set aside in refrigerator. Place wings in a re-sealable plastic bag. Pour remaining three-quarters of mixture into bag over wings. Seal bag and refrigerate 3 hours. Turn bag several times while marinating to coat wings evenly.

2. Spray grill grates with no-stick cooking spray. Prepare grill to medium-direct heat. Remove wings from bag and place on grill. Grill wings on each side basting frequently with set aside marinade until done. Internal temperature of wings should be at least 165°.

3. Transfer wings from grill to a platter. Cover with aluminum foil until ready to serve. Serve with blue cheese dip. See blue cheese dip recipes in appendix.

NOTES:

Date: _____

RATE THIS RECIPE
○ ○ ○ ○ ○

DIJON / MANGO / HONEY WINGS

Oven

		INGREDIENTS	SUBSTITUTIONS
☐	12	wings segmented, tips discarded – rinsed/dried	
☐	¼	cup Dijon mustard	_____
☐	½	cup mango chutney	_____
☐	¼	cup honey	_____
☐	2	tablespoons cider vinegar	_____
☐	¾	tablespoon ground ginger	_____
☐	2	garlic cloves – minced	_____
☐	1	teaspoon curry powder	_____
☐	¼	teaspoon cayenne pepper	_____
☐	¼	teaspoon salt	_____

1. Combine all ingredients except wings in a bowl and blend until mixture is smooth. Taste, adjust flavoring.

2. Line a large jelly roll baking pan with aluminum foil and coat liberally with no-stick cooking spray. Place oven rack in middle position. Preheat oven to 350°. Place wings on pan and bake wings 20 minutes.

3. Remove wings from oven and place in bowl with mango mixture. Coat thoroughly and return wings to pan. Continue to bake 10 – 20 minutes until done. Internal temperature of wings should be at least 165°.

4. Serve with blue cheese dip. See blue cheese dip recipes in appendix.

NOTES: Date: _____

RATE THIS RECIPE
○ ○ ○ ○ ○

GARLIC / HONEY WINGS

Marinate | Oven

		INGREDIENTS	SUBSTITUTIONS
☐	12	wings segmented, tips discarded – rinsed/dried	
☐	½	teaspoon salt	_____
☐	½	teaspoon black pepper	_____
☐	5	garlic cloves – minced	_____
☐	1	cup honey	_____
☐	½	tablespoon Worcestershire sauce	_____
☐	⅓	cup molasses	_____
☐	4	tablespoons soy sauce	_____

1. Season wings with salt and black pepper. Combine all ingredients except wings in a saucepan and bring mixture to a boil. Cool. Taste, adjust flavoring.

2. Place wings in a re-sealable plastic bag. Pour three-quarters of cooled honey mixture into bag and seal. Toss to coat thoroughly. Place remaining mixture in a bowl, cover and set aside in refrigerator until needed for basting. Marinate wings in refrigerator 3 hours. Turn bag at least once.

3. Place oven rack in middle position and preheat oven to 350°. Line a large jelly roll baking pan with aluminum foil and coat with no-stick cooking spray. Place wings on pan and spoon marinade over wings. Bake wings 20 minutes. Remove pan from oven. Turn wings and baste with set aside marinade. Bake additional 10 – 20 minutes until done. Internal temperature of wings should be at least 165°.

4. Serve with blue cheese dip. See blue cheese dip recipes in appendix.

NOTES:

Date: _____

RATE THIS RECIPE

○ ○ ○ ○ ○

HONEY / BARBECUE SAUCE GRILLED WINGS
Marinate | Grill

		INGREDIENTS	SUBSTITUTIONS
☐	12	wings segmented, tips discarded – rinsed/dried	
☐	½	tablespoon black pepper	_____
☐	1	tablespoon onion powder	_____
☐	1	tablespoon chili powder	_____
☐	1	tablespoon garlic powder	_____
☐	½	teaspoon salt	_____
☐	1	cup hickory wood chips	_____
☐	1	cup honey	_____
☐	½	cup hot barbecue sauce	_____
☐	3	tablespoons apple juice	_____

1. Combine black pepper, onion powder, chili powder, garlic powder and salt in a large re-sealable plastic bag and mix thoroughly. Taste, adjust flavoring. Add wings and toss to coat well. Seal and refrigerate 3 hours.

2. Spray grill grate with no-stick cooking spray. Prepare grill for low-indirect heat. Wings should not be placed directly over heat. Sprinkle ½ cup of hickory chips on coals. Grill wings 20 minutes. Sprinkle remaining chips over coals. Turn wings and grill another 20 minutes.

3. Combine honey, barbecue sauce and apple juice together in a saucepan. Cook over medium heat to a near boil.

4. Place wings on a baking sheet and pour sauce over wings. Toss to coat evenly. Grill wings until done. Internal temperature of wings should be at least 165°.

NOTES: Date: _____

RATE THIS RECIPE
○ ○ ○ ○ ○

HONEY / KETCHUP WINGS
Marinate | Oven

		INGREDIENTS	SUBSTITUTIONS
☐	12	wings segmented, tips discarded – rinsed/dried	
☐	¼	cup honey	_____
☐	¼	cup ketchup	_____
☐	2	tablespoons Worcestershire sauce	_____
☐	½	teaspoon onion powder	_____
☐	1	tablespoon soy sauce	_____
☐	1	tablespoon hot pepper sauce	_____
☐	1	teaspoon paprika	_____
☐	½	teaspoon salt	_____
☐	½	teaspoon black pepper	_____

1. Place wings in a re-sealable plastic bag. Combine honey, ketchup, Worcestershire, onion powder, soy sauce, hot pepper sauce and paprika in a bowl and mix well. Taste, adjust flavoring. Pour two-thirds of mixture over wings in plastic bag. Cover bowl and set aside remaining third of mixture in refrigerator until needed for basting wings. Seal bag, refrigerate and marinate wings 3 hours. Turn bag occasionally to coat wings evenly.

2. Place oven rack in middle position and preheat oven to 350°. Line a large jelly roll baking pan with aluminum foil and coat liberally with no-stick cooking spray. Place wings on pan and season with salt and black pepper. Bake wings 20 minutes. Remove wings from oven, turn and baste wings with reserved marinade. Bake additional 10 – 20 minutes until done. Internal temperature of wings should be at least 165°.

3. Remove pan from oven, platter wings and cover with aluminum foil until ready to serve.

NOTES: Date: _____

RATE THIS RECIPE
○ ○ ○ ○ ○

JAMAICAN HONEY WINGS

Oven

INGREDIENTS	SUBSTITUTIONS
☐ 12 wings segmented, tips discarded – rinsed/dried	
☐ 2 tablespoons extra virgin olive oil	_____
☐ 2 tablespoons ground ginger	_____
☐ ½ cup honey	_____
☐ ¼ cup sherry	_____
☐ ¼ cup cider vinegar	_____
☐ 2 tablespoons sesame oil	_____
☐ 3 tablespoons soy sauce	_____
☐ 2 garlic cloves – minced	_____
☐ ½ teaspoon chili powder	_____

1. Put oil and ginger in a large saucepan. Cook 2 minutes over medium heat. Add honey, sherry, vinegar, sesame oil, soy sauce, garlic and chili powder and cook 2 minutes. Taste, adjust flavoring. Transfer sauce to a large bowl.

2. Place oven rack in middle position and preheat oven to 350°. Line a large jelly roll baking pan with aluminum foil and coat liberally with no-stick cooking spray. Place wings on pan and spoon three-quarters of sauce over wings. Remaining sauce is to be used for basting after baking wings.

3. Bake wings in oven 20 minutes. Turn wings and baste with pan juices. Bake additional 10 – 20 minutes until done. Internal temperature of wings should be at least 165°. Brush wings with remaining quarter of sauce.

4. Remove wings with a slotted spoon, platter and cover with aluminum foil until ready to serve.

NOTES: Date: _____

RATE THIS RECIPE
○ ○ ○ ○ ○

LIME / HONEY WINGS

Marinate | Oven

	INGREDIENTS	SUBSTITUTIONS
☐	12 wings segmented, tips discarded – rinsed/dried	
☐	½ cup honey	_____
☐	¼ cup lime juice	_____
☐	¼ cup grated lime zest	_____
☐	4 garlic cloves – minced	_____
☐	½ teaspoon salt	_____
☐	½ teaspoon black pepper	_____

1. Mix together honey, lime juice, lime zest, garlic, salt and black pepper in a large bowl and mix well. Taste, adjust flavoring.

2. Place wings in a re-sealable plastic bag. Add half of marinade to bag, seal and refrigerate wings 3 hours. Turn bag occasionally to coat wings evenly. Cover and refrigerate other half of marinade in a bowl to use as a coating after cooking.

3. Place oven rack in middle position and preheat oven to 350°. Line a large jelly roll baking pan with aluminum foil and coat liberally with no-stick cooking spray. Place wings on pan. Spoon marinade from bag over wings. Bake 20 minutes.

4. Remove pan from oven, turn wings and baste with pan juices. Bake additional 10 – 20 minutes until done. Internal temperature of wings should be at least 165°. Bring reserved marinade bowl from refrigerator to room temperature. Place wings in bowl and toss to coat completely. Remove wings with a slotted spoon, platter and cover with aluminum foil until ready to serve.

NOTES:

Date: _____

RATE THIS RECIPE
○ ○ ○ ○ ○

MOLASSES / HONEY WINGS
Marinate | Oven

INGREDIENTS	SUBSTITUTIONS
☐ 12 wings segmented, tips discarded – rinsed/dried	
☐ ½ cup molasses	_____
☐ ½ cup honey	_____
☐ ½ cup soy sauce	_____
☐ 3 garlic cloves – minced	_____
☐ ½ teaspoon paprika	_____
☐ ¼ teaspoon salt	_____
☐ ¼ teaspoon black pepper	_____
☐ 2 tablespoons chili sauce	_____
☐ 1 teaspoon ground ginger	_____

1. Place all ingredients except wings in a large bowl and blend thoroughly. Place wings in a re-sealable plastic bag. Add mixture to bag. Toss to coat thoroughly. Seal bag and refrigerate 3 hours. Turn wings at least once.

2. Place oven rack in middle position and preheat oven to 350°. Line a large jelly roll baking pan with aluminum foil and coat with no-stick cooking spray. Place wings on pan and spoon marinade over wings.

3. Bake wings 20 minutes. Remove pan from oven, turn wings and baste with pan juices. Bake additional 10 – 20 minutes until done. Internal temperature of wings should be at least 165°.

4. Remove pan from oven, platter wings and cover with aluminum foil until ready to serve.

NOTES:

Date: _____

RATE THIS RECIPE
○ ○ ○ ○ ○

RANCH / BLUE CHEESE / HONEY WINGS
Marinate | Oven

		INGREDIENTS	SUBSTITUTIONS
☐	12	wings segmented, tips discarded – rinsed/dried	
☐	2	tablespoons honey	_____
☐	2	tablespoons ketchup	_____
☐	1	tablespoon hot pepper sauce	_____
☐	1	teaspoon paprika	_____
☐	1	tablespoon Worcestershire sauce	_____
☐	½	cup ranch dressing	_____
☐	¼	cup blue cheese dressing	_____
☐	1	teaspoon soy sauce	_____

1. Place honey, ketchup, hot pepper sauce, paprika and Worcestershire in a bowl and mix thoroughly. Taste, adjust flavoring. Place wings in a re-sealable plastic bag. Pour mixture into bag. Seal, refrigerate and marinate 3 hour. Turn bag occasionally to coat wings.

2. Place oven rack in middle position and heat oven to 350°. Line a large jelly roll baking pan with aluminum foil and coat liberally with no-stick cooking spray. Place wings on pan. Spoon some mixture over wings.

3. Bake 20 minutes. Remove pan from oven, turn wings and baste with pan juices. Bake additional 10 – 20 minutes until done. Internal temperature of wings should be at least 165°.

4. Combine ranch dressing, blue cheese dressing and soy sauce in a bowl.

5. Remove pan from oven, platter wings and cover with aluminum foil until ready to serve. Serve wings with ranch/blue cheese dressing mixture.

NOTES: Date: _____

WING
DIPPING SAUCES

BLACK BEAN DIP

INGREDIENTS | SUBSTITUTIONS

- ☐ ½ cup cooked black beans – drained
- ☐ ¼ cup prepared salsa verde
- ☐ ¼ cup sour cream
- ☐ 1 tablespoon lime juice
- ☐ 2 teaspoons hot pepper sauce
- ☐ 2 teaspoons fresh cilantro – chopped
- ☐ ½ teaspoon salt

Instructions. Combine all ingredients in a blender. Cover and blend until smooth. Store dip, covered, in the refrigerator until ready to serve.

BLUE CHEESE / CREAM DIP

INGREDIENTS | SUBSTITUTIONS

- ☐ 1 cup blue cheese – crumbled
- ☐ ½ cup mayonnaise
- ☐ ½ cup buttermilk
- ☐ 3 tablespoons half-and-half
- ☐ 2 teaspoons Worcestershire sauce
- ☐ ½ teaspoon salt
- ☐ ¼ teaspoon black pepper
- ☐ milk – tablespoons as needed

Instructions. Combine all ingredients in a blender. Cover and blend until smooth. Add enough milk to give sauce consistency of pancake batter. Store dip, covered, in the refrigerator for up to 2 weeks. If desired, top dip with additional crumbled blue cheese before serving.

BLUE CHEESE DIP

INGREDIENTS | SUBSTITUTIONS
- ☐ ½ cup blue cheese – crumbled _____
- ☐ ¼ cup whipped cream cheese _____
- ☐ ⅓ cup sour cream _____
- ☐ 2 garlic cloves – minced _____
- ☐ 1 teaspoon Worcestershire sauce _____
- ☐ ½ teaspoon salt _____
- ☐ ¼ teaspoon black pepper _____
- ☐ milk – tablespoons as needed _____

Instructions. Combine all ingredients in a blender. Cover and blend until smooth. Add enough milk to give sauce consistency of pancake batter. Store dip, covered, in the refrigerator for up to 2 weeks. If desired, top dip with additional crumbled blue cheese before serving.

BLUE CHEESE / HOT SAUCE DIP

INGREDIENTS | SUBSTITUTIONS
- ☐ 8 ounces blue cheese – crumbled _____
- ☐ ½ cup sour cream _____
- ☐ ¼ cup whipped cream cheese _____
- ☐ 1 teaspoon hot pepper sauce _____
- ☐ ½ teaspoon salt _____
- ☐ ¼ teaspoon black pepper _____
- ☐ ½ teaspoon Worcestershire sauce _____
- ☐ milk – tablespoons as needed _____

Instructions. Combine all ingredients in a blender. Cover and blend until smooth. Add enough milk to give sauce consistency of pancake batter. Store dip, covered, in the refrigerator for up to 2 weeks. If desired, top dip with additional crumbled blue cheese before serving.

BLUE CHEESE / LEMON JUICE DIP

	INGREDIENTS	SUBSTITUTIONS
☐	½ cup blue cheese – crumbled	_____
☐	¾ cup mayonnaise	_____
☐	½ cup sour cream	_____
☐	2 garlic cloves – minced	_____
☐	2 teaspoons chopped parsley	_____
☐	1 teaspoon lemon juice	_____
☐	1 teaspoon cider vinegar	_____
☐	¼ teaspoon salt	_____
☐	¼ teaspoon black pepper	_____
☐	milk – tablespoons as needed	_____

Instructions.
Combine all ingredients in a blender. Cover and blend until smooth. Add enough milk to give sauce consistency of pancake batter. Store dip, covered, in the refrigerator for up to 2 weeks. If desired, top dip with additional crumbled blue cheese before serving.

BLUE CHEESE / ONION / GARLIC DIP

INGREDIENTS   SUBSTITUTIONS

- ☐ 6 ounces blue cheese – crumbled   _____
- ☐ ¼ stick butter   _____
- ☐ 1 small onion – finely chopped   _____
- ☐ 2 garlic cloves – minced   _____
- ☐ 7 ounces mayonnaise   _____
- ☐ ¼ pint sour cream   _____
- ☐ 2 tablespoons lemon juice   _____
- ☐ 2 tablespoons freshly chopped parsley   _____
- ☐ ¾ teaspoon chili powder   _____
- ☐ 1 teaspoon cumin   _____
- ☐ ¼ teaspoon salt   _____
- ☐ ¼ teaspoon black pepper   _____
- ☐ milk – tablespoons as needed   _____

Instructions. Melt butter in a sauce pan. Combine all ingredients in a blender. Cover and blend until smooth. Add enough milk to give sauce consistency of pancake batter. Store dip, covered, in the refrigerator for up to 2 weeks. If desired, top dip with additional crumbled blue cheese before serving.

BLUE CHEESE / SCALLION DIP

INGREDIENTS

SUBSTITUTIONS

- ☐ ¾ cup blue cheese – crumbled
- ☐ ½ cup mayonnaise
- ☐ ¼ cup whipped cream cheese
- ☐ 1 teaspoon cider vinegar
- ☐ 2 scallions including green tops – chopped
- ☐ ¼ teaspoon salt
- ☐ ¼ teaspoon black pepper
- ☐ milk – tablespoons as needed

Instructions.
Combine all ingredients in a blender. Cover and blend until smooth. Add enough milk to give sauce consistency of pancake batter. Store dip, covered, in the refrigerator for up to 2 weeks. If desired, top dip with additional crumbled blue cheese before serving.

BLUE CHEESE / WORCESTERSHIRE DIP

	INGREDIENTS	SUBSTITUTIONS
☐ 3	tablespoons blue cheese – crumbled	_____
☐ ½	cup cottage cheese	_____
☐ ½	teaspoon white wine vinegar	_____
☐ 1	tablespoon white pepper	_____
☐ 2	garlic cloves – minced	_____
☐ 1	teaspoon Worcestershire sauce	_____
☐ ¼	teaspoon salt	_____
☐ ¼	teaspoon black pepper	_____
☐	milk – tablespoons as needed	_____

Instructions. Combine all ingredients in a blender. Cover and blend until smooth. Add enough milk to give sauce consistency of pancake batter. Store dip, covered, in the refrigerator for up to 2 weeks. If desired, top dip with additional crumbled blue cheese before serving.

CUCUMBER DIP

		INGREDIENTS	SUBSTITUTIONS
☐	1	medium cucumber – seeded and chopped fine	
☐	¼	cup sour cream	_____
☐	¼	cup whipped cream cheese	_____
☐	½	cup mayonnaise	_____
☐	⅓	cup minced fresh coriander	_____
☐	¼	teaspoon salt	_____
☐	¼	teaspoon black pepper	_____
☐	1	teaspoon fresh lemon juice	_____
☐		milk – tablespoons as needed	_____

Instructions. Combine all ingredients in a blender. Cover and blend until smooth. Add enough milk to give sauce consistency of pancake batter. Store dip, covered, in the refrigerator for up to 2 weeks. If desired, top dip with additional cucumber before serving.

HERB / CITRUS SAUCE DIP

		INGREDIENTS	SUBSTITUTIONS
☐	2	flat-leaf parsley leaves	
☐	1	jalapeño pepper – ribs and seeds removed – chopped	
☐	2	tablespoons lime juice	
☐	1	garlic clove – chopped	
☐	½	teaspoon salt	
☐	½	teaspoon black pepper	
☐	¼	cup extra virgin olive oil	
☐	2	tablespoons heavy cream	

Instructions. Combine all ingredients in a blender. Cover and blend until smooth. Store dip, covered, in the refrigerator until ready to serve.

MAYONNAISE DIP

		INGREDIENTS	SUBSTITUTIONS
☐	1	cup mayonnaise	
☐	½	cup sour cream	
☐	1	tablespoon Dijon mustard	
☐	2	chipotle chilies in adobo – drained & minced	
☐	1	tablespoon adobo sauce	
☐		milk – tablespoons as needed	
☐	½	teaspoon salt	
☐	½	teaspoon black pepper	

Instructions. Combine all ingredients in a blender. Cover and blend until smooth. Add enough milk to give sauce consistency of pancake batter. Store dip, covered, in the refrigerator for up to 2 weeks.

NOTES

NOTES

APPENDIX

PLAYING WITH FIRE (INSIDE)

There are numerous methods for applying heat to food, thus turning it from tartar to terrific. Below are tips and tricks for effectively and safely performing this common-place yet profound metamorphosis indoors.

OVEN COOKING

Consider these tips:

- Oven mitts are mandatory and should always be kept where they are easily accessible. You run the risk of serious injury if you forget to glove your hand before thrusting said hand into the inferno of the oven and grabbing a hot handle.

- Preheating the oven is essential when following recommended cooking temperatures in recipes. If the oven is not at the recommended temp when you begin cooking the dish, the results may be less than palatable.

- Place the oven racks in the proper position before you preheat the oven. If you wait to move the rack after heating, you will be moving a hot oven rack and could potentially burn yourself.

- Double check the temperature settings before placing the dish in the oven.

- Utensils need to be ovenproof. If the tool is not ovenproof, it may melt when placed in a hot oven.

- When oven cooking with a sheet pan or broiling pan, line it with aluminum foil first. Spray the foil with no-stick cooking oil. Using foil will protect the pan from baked-on ingredients. Recipes with sugar products—white sugar, brown sugar, maple syrup, corn syrup or molasses—will burn hard onto the pan surface if it is not protected, sometimes to the point where it is easier to throw the pan out than clean it.

- Some recipes call for cooking the dish both covered and uncovered at different times in the cooking process. For best results, follow the instructions carefully.

Oven temperatures are often classified into categories. Here are the distinctions that I like to use:

250° – 300°	Low
301° – 350°	Medium
351° – 425°	Hot
426° – 475°	Very Hot
476° plus	Whatcha got yourself there, a nuclear reactor?

STOVE TOP COOKING

- The best stove top cooking happens when the correct size burner is used. Use small pots, pans and skillets on the small burners, and larger vessels on the larger burners.

- Make sure the temperature setting is correct. A high setting when the recipe calls for a low setting will ruin a dish quickly.

- Keep cooking utensils and ingredients in a location that won't require reaching across the burners or cooking vessels.

- When braising or sautéing food in a saucepan, the splattering of the butter or oil can cause serious burns. To minimize that chance, slightly lift the edge of the skillet that is closest to you and work with the ingredients at the back of the skillet.

- Consider when a lid cover or a splatter screen might be useful. Both minimize grease splatters, protecting you from burns. Bonus: will help keep the stove top and counters clean.

SLOW COOKER / CROCK-POT COOKING

The terms "slow cooker" and "crock-pot" are synonymous and refer to the same hardware. The lowest setting is generally about 200° and the high setting is about 300°. One cooking hour on high is roughly equivalent to two cooking hours on low. Many recipes that call for the "low" setting will go for approximately 8 hours, and if the recipes calls for "high," it is a good bet the recommended cooking time will be 3 – 4 hours.

To obtain the best dishes, the slow cooker must be no more than two-thirds full. Half full is fine. Steam creates a vacuum that seals the lid and the lid needs a tight fit to form a vacuum. If filled to the brim, the top will most likely not seal correctly.

Opening the lid prolongs the cooking time. Each time you remove the lid, it can add up to 15 minutes to the cooking time.

Some recipes suggest stirring the dish halfway through cooking. Stir quickly and replace the lid quickly.

Here are some tips for producing successful slow cooker dishes:

- Selecting cheaper cuts of meat is actually preferable when using a slow cooker. They have less fat, and the long, moist cooking turns what are normally tough cuts into tender treats.

- Remove poultry skin and excess fat. The fat melts with the slow cooking process and adds a distinctly unpleasant flavor and texture to the dish.

- Cut meat and poultry into cube pieces. This will ensure thorough cooking.

- Defrost foods before cooking.

- Foods at the bottom of the crock-pot cook at slightly higher temperatures. Pay attention to this when loading the vessel. For instance, when cooking a dish with meat and root vegetables, placing the vegetables on the bottom and the meat on top will help all the ingredients come to doneness at the same time.

- To ramp up the flavors, the liquid can be concentrated by cranking the slow cooker up to high for the last half hour.

- To prevent dairy products (sour cream, heavy cream, yogurt, milk) from breaking down, add during the last 15 minutes of cooking.

- The ceramic insert of the slow cooker can be damaged by sudden temperature changes. It should not be immersed in water while still hot from cooking, or taken from the refrigerator and placed into a preheated base.

- Exercise care when cleaning the ceramic insert. Let the insert cool before immersing it in water. Use a soft cloth and warm, soapy water to clean the insert. Do not use any harsh cleaners or abrasive cleansing pads. Do not immerse the slow cooker heating element or the cord in water, and keep the unit unplugged when not in use.

DEEP FRYING

Deep frying wings at home, inside, can be an exhilarating, adventurous, delicious experience. It can also lead to burns, serious disfigurement, a burnt shell of a home, or worse. Exercise extraordinary caution when deep frying at home.

- You must use an oil with a high smoke point. Peanut oil and canola oil are the two best choices, even perhaps the only choices. We are trying to prevent fire here, after all.

- A deep, very heavy skillet or a deep fat fryer specifically designed for the purpose should be used. Add oil only to the recommended level, no higher. With skillets, fill no higher than two inches from the top. This will allow for spattering of the oil as the wings are added.

- Bring the raw wings to room temperature and make sure they are clean and dry. Bring the temperature of the oil to approximately 360° - 375°, using a high temperature oil thermometer to confirm.

- Add a few wings at a time and allow the oil temperature to return to cooking temperature before adding more wings. If you add too many wings at once, the oil temperature will fall dramatically. If the oil temperature is low, the wings will cook poorly, absorb more oil and taste greasy.

- Leave plenty of space between the wings to allow them to cook evenly. Fry the wings in the oil until they are golden brown. Wings are done when they reach an internal temperature of at least 165°, using a meat thermometer to confirm.

- Remove the wings with a long handled slotted spoon and drain on a plate covered with a double thickness of paper towels. You can place the cooked wings in a bowl and keep them warm in a 250° oven.

- Moderate reuse of oil is acceptable, meaning one or two more uses. Always allow the oil to cool completely before handling— generally it takes about two hours. Be sure to strain the cool oil before reusing.

- Never, *never* attempt to put out a grease fire with water. You will only cause the oil to erupt and this will spread the fire around the kitchen, and, in all probability, throughout the house. Use a dry chemical Class B extinguisher.[1] (Most household fire extinguishers are Class ABC, so are appropriate.) Use large amounts of salt or large amounts of baking soda to extinguish the fire if an extinguisher is not available.

PLAYING WITH FIRE (OUTSIDE)

There is something primal about grilling food outdoors. The open air, the billowing fragrant smoke, the constant tending of the grill temperature, and the elaborate, almost ritual poking and prodding of the food. Below are tips and tricks for maximizing the grilling experience that have worked for me over the years.

ABOUT COALS

Open the vents on the bottom of the grill. Light a large chimney starter full of charcoal. If you don't own a chimney starter, I highly recommend you acquire one. When the coals are glowing grayish white (start checking coals after 15 minutes), the coals are at their hottest. Spread the coals on the lower grate.

Positioning coals is critical for controlling the grill heat. Use long handled tongs to spread the coals around the lower grate. Leave a little space between coals.

THREE GRILLING METHODS

Here are three different tried-and-true grilling methods that are effective for just about any grilling situation. The methods are direct heat, indirect heat and tri-divided heat.

DIRECT HEAT

For even temperature distribution, spread the coals uniformly over the coal grate, at a depth of one or two coals. Open the bottom vents. Open the top vents if grilling with the cover on.

INDIRECT HEAT

This is the best method for barbecuing or slow roasting. The cooking is done with the grill covered and the meat grilled for an extended period, sometimes with wood chips to impart a smoked flavor.

Place an aluminum drip pan in the center of the charcoal grate. Light the coals and, when the coals are covered with gray ash, place the coals around the drip pan. Water can be added to the pan to provide moisture. Do not place meat directly over coals when grilling with indirect heat.

The temperature of the grill can be controlled by manipulating the upper and lower vents. The temperature for low-indirect cooking should be kept at approximately 275° for the entire cooking period. Use a grill thermometer to determine actual temperatures.

If you are using wood chips, leave the cover slightly ajar to draw smoke upward over the meat.

TRI-DIVIDED HEAT

The third grilling method is to divide the coal grate into three sections. Place the coals that will provide the heat area for searing in section one, to the far left. The second section is a coal-free cooking area in the center, next to the burning coals. When grilling in the second section, the meat will not be directly above the coals. The third section of the grill is also coal-free and has less heat and is some distance from the coals. This is a good area for resting meats, and is an area to move the meat in the event of flare-ups.

GRILL HEAT CONTROL

Avoid lifting the grill cover too often. When the cover is lifted, the temperature drops significantly and the cooking time is extended. Use a grill thermometer to determine actual grill temperature.

HEAT TOO HIGH

If grill heat is too high, there are actions that can be taken to reduce the heat. The first is to use long handled tongs to scatter coals. Move the food to the coolest section of the grill. The vents, top and bottom, should be closed or nearly closed to starve the charcoal of oxygen.

HEAT TOO LOW

If the heat is too low, there are several things you can do to increase the heat. The first is to consolidate the coals by stacking them all in one place and adding more charcoal, preheated if possible. If the coals are not pre-heated, place the fresh coals on the hot collection of coals. Fan the coals with a newspaper. Lastly, open all the vents to provide plenty of oxygen.

If you are in a northern climate during the winter, clear the grill of any snow and provide more time for preheating. Increase the recommended cooking temperature by 15% – 20% to allow for the chill. Do not grill in an enclosed environment such as a basement or garage as deadly carbon monoxide gases can be trapped.

GAS GRILLS

Preheat all burners on high, cover the grill with the lid and heat for 10 minutes and then adjust heat according to recipe. For indirect heat cooking, turn off one burner. Turn off the middle burner if there are three. Always have a backup tank of gas.

GRILL SAFETY

- Place the grill well away from existing structures, deck railings, house eaves and trees.

- Place the grill a safe distance from other activities, especially foot traffic.

- Grills are designed to be used out-of-doors only. Indoor use poses both a fire hazard and the risk of carbon monoxide exposure.

- Always use long-handled grilling tools to give you plenty of clearance from heat and flames when cooking.

- Excess grease buildup in your grill is a fire hazard and will contribute to flare-ups while cooking, if not outright fire. Be sure to clean your grill periodically.

AVOIDING THE EMERGENCY ROOM

RUDE POISONING

Food poisoning (Food Borne Illness) is nasty and potentially deadly. Most preventable cases of food poisoning are caused by cross-contamination from raw meat, poultry, seafood and dairy products (a.k.a. "proteins").

Food safety issues occur when food is between the temperatures of 40° and 140° – the Food Danger Zone. Cooked food should never be allowed to remain in the danger zone for more than a couple of hours at most. Foods in the danger zone are a breeding ground for the bacteria and other toxins responsible for food-borne illnesses.

If food poisoning occurs in your home, take note of the foods eaten and then freeze any uneaten portions. The frozen samples may need to be tested in order to identify the offending bug and appropriate medical treatment.

When safety of the protein is in doubt, *discard it*. Always err on the side of safety.

SAFE HANDLING OF PROTEINS

- Refrigerate proteins promptly after purchase.
- Raw proteins should never be left out at room temperature.
- Packaged proteins can be refrigerated in the original packaging.
- Freeze uncooked proteins if they will not be used within 2 days.
- Proteins will take from 4 – 10 hours to thaw in the refrigerator. Do not thaw proteins on the counter top.
- To thaw proteins in cold water, place in a watertight plastic bag and change water frequently.
- The microwave can be used to thaw most proteins. Thawing seafood in the microwave is not recommended.

- Frozen, uncooked proteins such as meat and poultry should be used within two or three months of freezing. Frozen cooked protein should be used within a month of freezing. Freezing seafood – cooked or uncooked – is not recommended unless it is professionally frozen.

AVOIDING CROSS-CONTAMINATION

- Uncooked protein should be kept separate from produce, cooked foods and ready-to-eat foods.

- Never place cooked food on a plate that previously held uncooked protein.

- If you intend to use the marinade as a sauce, (1) keep a portion of the unused marinade separate for use on the cooked protein, or (2) place the used marinade in a sauce pan and bring it to a boil. Reduce heat and simmer for 4 – 5 minutes.

- Use one cutting board for fresh produce, such as vegetables and fruits, and a different one for raw proteins. If you must use only one cutting board, wash it thoroughly with hot, soapy water after using with raw proteins.

- Using hot soapy water, wash your hands, dishes, knives and other utensils thoroughly after coming in contact with uncooked proteins. For cutting boards and counters, use a hot soapy water scrub followed by a rinse solution of one tablespoon liquid bleach to one gallon water. Rinse with water.

COOKING TEMPERATURES

Cooking times listed in recipes are approximations. A meat thermometer is a necessary piece of cooking equipment for ensuring the proper internal temperature of foods. Always use this critical piece of cooking hardware to monitor internal temperatures.

See Table 5 in the Appendix[1] for recommended safe internal temperatures for cooked meats.

STOP, DROP AND ROLL

Cooking is the leading cause of home fires and home fire injuries in the United States. Taking proper precautions and learning what to do in case of a kitchen fire can prevent property damage, injury, and potentially save lives.

- Do not leave pots and pans unattended on the stove or in the oven. Most home fires are the result of unattended cooking. Turn pan handles on the stove towards the back to prevent food spills or children accidentally grabbing the handles.

- Pot holders and towels should be kept away from stove tops and ovens. Bathrobes, aprons and loose clothing are highly susceptible to catching fire. If clothing catches fire, immediately stop, drop to the ground and roll to smother the fire.

- In case of fire, turn off the burner under the burning pot or pan. Cover the fire with a large lid. Leave the lid on until the pan cools. Turn off the hood fan so fire is not drawn into the ducts.

- Always, *always* have a properly rated fire extinguisher within arms reach. Familiarize yourself with the instructions and practice a dry-run so you can operate it if and when needed.

- Never, *never* attempt to put out a grease fire with water. You will only cause the oil to erupt and this will spread the fire around the kitchen, and, in all probability, throughout the house. Use a Class B extinguisher.[2] (Most household fire extinguishers are Class ABC, so are appropriate.)

- Call 911 in the event of a fire..

TABLES

TABLE 1: HERB AND SPICE SUBSTITUTIONS

RECIPE CALLS FOR	OPTION 1	OPTION 2
Allspice	cinnamon with a dash of nutmeg	dash of cloves
Basil	oregano	thyme
Cajun Spice	combine white pepper, garlic powder, onion powder, ground red pepper, paprika and black pepper	
Chili Powder	dashes of hot pepper sauce, oregano and cumin	
Chive	green onion	leek
Cilantro	parsley	
Italian Seasoning	blend of basil, oregano, rosemary and ground red pepper	
Cinnamon	nutmeg	allspice
Cloves	cinnamon	nutmeg
Cumin	chili powder	
Garlic, 1 clove	¼ teaspoon garlic powder	½ teaspoon prepared minced garlic
Ginger	allspice	cinnamon
Horseradish, 1 tablespoon fresh	2 tablespoons bottled	
Hot pepper sauce, 1 teaspoon	¾ teaspoon cayenne pepper plus 1 teaspoon vinegar	
Marjoram	basil	thyme
Mustard prepared, 1 tablespoon	1 teaspoon dry mustard	
Mustard dry, 1 teaspoon	1 tablespoon prepared mustard	

RECIPE CALLS FOR	OPTION 1	OPTION 2
Mustard Dijon, 1 tablespoon	1 tablespoon dry mustard mixed with 1 teaspoon white wine vinegar, 1 tablespoon mayonnaise, and a pinch of sugar	
Nutmeg	cinnamon	ginger
Oregano	thyme	basil
Parsley, ¼ cup chopped fresh	1 tablespoon dried parsley flakes	¼ cup chopped cilantro
Poultry Seasoning	sage plus a blend of thyme, marjoram, black pepper, and rosemary	
Red Pepper	dash of hot pepper sauce	black pepper
Rosemary	thyme	tarragon
Sage	poultry seasoning	marjoram
Thyme	basil	oregano

TABLE 2: COMMON INGREDIENT SUBSTITUTIONS

RECIPE CALLS FOR	ALTERNATIVE
Broth, beef or chicken, 1 cup	1 bouillon cube dissolved in 1 cup boiling water
Coconut milk, 1 cup	3 tablespoons canned cream of coconut plus enough milk to equal 1 cup
Cornstarch, 1 tablespoon	2 tablespoon all-purpose flour
Corn syrup	honey
Cream, half-and-half, 1 cup	½ cup whole milk, plus ½ cup light cream
Cream cheese	cottage cheese, puréed
Green onions	onion
Honey, 1 cup	1¼ cups sugar plus ¼ cup liquid
Leeks	shallots
Lemon juice	vinegar
Maple syrup, 2 cups	honey, 1 cup
Mayonnaise, 1 cup	½ cup yogurt and ½ cup mayonnaise
Mushrooms, 1 pound fresh	6 ounces canned mushrooms
Oil (sauteing), ¼ cup	¼ cup melted butter
Onion, 1 medium	1 tablespoon dried minced onion
Red Pepper	dash of hot pepper sauce
Sour cream, 1 cup	1 cup sour milk and ¼ cup butter
Sugar brown, 1 cup firmly packed	1 cup granulated sugar plus ¼ cup unsulphured molasses
Tomatoes, 1 cup canned	1½ cups chopped tomato, simmered for 10 minutes
Tomato juice, 1 cup	½ cup tomato sauce plus ½ cup water
Tomato ketchup	1 cup tomato sauce plus ½ cup sugar and 2 tablespoons vinegar
Tomato sauce, 2 cups	¾ cup tomato paste plus 1 cup water
Vinegar, Balsamic	sherry vinegar
Vinegar (white or cider)	lemon juice
Worcestershire sauce	bottled steak sauce

TABLE 3: HEALTHY INGREDIENT SUBSTITUTIONS

RECIPE CALLS FOR	HEALTHY ALTERNATIVE
Bacon	turkey bacon, ham, Canadian bacon
Butter	60/40 butter blend with reduced calorie margarine
Cream	skim milk, evaporated skim milk
Cream cheese	yogurt cheese
Egg, 1 whole	2 egg whites
Egg, 2 whole	1 whole egg plus 2 egg whites
Ground beef	ground poultry
Heavy cream, 1 cup	1 tablespoon flour whisked into 1 cup nonfat milk
Mayonnaise	half light mayonnaise and half non-fat yogurt
Meat	legumes, lentils, dried beans or dried peas
Milk, whole	2% milk, 1% milk, skim milk, evaporated milk or soy milk fortified with calcium
Sour cream, 1 cup	1 cup low fat cottage cheese plus 2 tablespoons skim milk plus 1 tablespoon lemon juice
Tuna, canned, oil-packed	canned tuna, water-packed
White bread	100% whole grain or 100% whole wheat bread

TABLE 4: LIQUOR SUBSTITUTIONS

RECIPE CALLS FOR	OPTION 1	OPTION 2
Amaretto	almond extract	marzipan
Apple brandy	apple juice	apple cider
Apricot brandy	apricot preserves	
Beer or Ale	chicken broth	ginger ale
Bourbon	sparkling grape juice	vanilla extract
Brandy	raspberry extract	brandy extract
Champagne	ginger ale	soda water
Cognac	peach juice	apricot juice
Coffee liqueur	espresso	coffee syrup
Creme de Menthe	grapefruit juice	mint extract
Grand Marnier	orange marmalade	orange juice
Peppermint Schnapps	mint extract	mint leaves
Port	cranberry juice plus lemon juice	
Rum	pineapple juice	vanilla extract
Sherry	apple cider	coffee syrup
Vermouth	apple cider	
Vodka	white grape juice plus lime juice	apple cider
Wine, Red	grape juice	cranberry juice
Wine, White	white grape juice	apple juice

TABLE 5: SAFE INTERNAL TEMPERATURES

CUT	MINIMUM SAFE INTERNAL TEMPERATURE
Roasts – Beef, veal, lamb	145° F (medium rare) 160° F (medium)
Fish, shellfish	145° F
Pork	160° F
Ground – beef, lamb, veal	160° F
Egg dishes	160° F
Poultry, any cut	165° F
Leftovers, any meat	165° F

TABLE 6: TRINITY FLAVOR BASES

TRINITY	1	2	3
French (Mirepoix)	celery	onion	carrots
Cajun or Creole (Holy Trinity - 1:2:3 ratio)	onion	bell pepper	celery
Italian	tomato	garlic	basil
Mexican	ancho chili pepper	pasilla chili pepper	guajillo chili pepper
Chinese	scallions	ginger	garlic
Greek	lemon juice	olive oil	oregano
Indian	garlic	ginger	onion
Spanish	garlic	onion	tomato
Thai	galangal	kaffir lime	lemon grass

TABLE 7: PEPPERHEAD SCALE

PEPPER	SCOVILLE HEAT UNITS
Cherry	500
Sonora	600
Coronado	1,000
Polano	2,000
Ancho	2,000
Anaheim	2,500
Chipotle	5,000
Jalapeño	10,000
Serrano	22,000
Tabasco	50,000
Cayenne	50,000
Jamaican Hot	200,000
Chocolate Habanero	425,000
Police Pepper Spray	5,300,000
Pure Capsaicin	16,000,000

TABLE 8: RECOMMENDED WING GEAR

GEAR	DESCRIPTION
Aluminum foil	12-inch wide works well for lining the baking pan and for covering the wings after cooking.
Baking pan	A rectangular baking pan is used for baking wings and sauces together. A heavy duty pan that will not warp works best.
Basting brush	A heavy 2-inch silicone brush with a comfortable 8-inch handle works well.
Extra bag of charcoal	Never run out, never say die
Extra LP tank	Never run out, never say die
Fire Extinguisher	One in the kitchen, one by the grill
Grill thermometer	Helpful for regulating grill temperature.
Heavy knife or heavy scissors	Used for cutting the wings segments. The heavier and sharper the knife the better. A rigid knife works well. An industrial-strength pair of scissors sometimes works better than a knife for segmenting wings.
Measuring cup	A measuring cup registering standard increments.
Measuring spoons	A complete set of measuring spoons from 1/8 teaspoon to a full tablespoon.
Meat thermometer	Essential for determining when the wings are ready to safely eat.
Mixing bowls	Various sizes used for mixing sauces and marinades.
Oven mitts	Used for protection when extracting items from the oven and when working the grill.
Re-sealable plastic bags	Used for coating and marinating wings.
Saucepans	Used for preparing sauce. Saucepans with heavy bottoms work best.
Short- and long-handled Tongs	Used for extracting wings from marinade and for turning wings when baking and grilling.

GEAR	DESCRIPTION
Skillets	Used for braising and sauce reduction – a large skillet for braising and a smaller one for sauces. I recommend a stainless steel skillet with an aluminum core.
Spatula	For stirring and coating wings. Spatulas with tips rigid and large enough to mix and coat a lot of wings at a time work best.

REFERENCES

[1] Excerpt from USDA Keep Food Safe! Food Safety Basics
http://www.fsis.usda.gov/factsheets/Keep_Food_Safe_Food_Safety_Basics/index.asp

[2] U.S. Fire Administration, Fire Extinguishers
http://www.usfa.dhs.gov/citizens/home_fire_prev/extinguishers.shtm

NOTES

INDEX

orange zest 41, 52, 92
oregano 104
oyster sauce 45

P

paprika 46, 47, 68, 73, 104, 106, 107, 121, 122, 126, 129, 130
parsley 137, 138, 142
peach chutney 83
peanut butter 109, 110, 111, 112
peanut oil 50, 56, 58, 103, 111, 112
peanuts, unsalted 114
picante sauce 84
pineapple 84
pineapple juice 34, 86, 88, 89
plum jam 91
plums 90
potato chips 104

R

ranch dressing 130
raspberry jam 93, 94
red chili flakes 43
red currant jelly 41
red pepper flakes 34, 40, 54, 80, 81, 112
red wine 34, 42, 43, 61, 108
red wine, dry 41
rice wine 117
root beer 44
rosemary 47, 56
rum, spiced 47

S

salsa 27, 54, 99, 135
scallions 107, 116, 117, 139
seasoned salt 34, 79
sesame oil 34, 40, 127
sesame seeds 72
sherry 46, 114, 127
sour cream 135, 136, 137, 138, 141, 142

soy sauce 28, 32, 34, 36, 38, 39, 40, 41, 42, 43, 44, 45, 46, 55, 58, 60, 61, 70, 72, 74, 76, 78, 80, 81, 84, 86, 89, 91, 92, 94, 100, 102, 106, 107, 108, 110, 111, 112, 114, 117, 121, 122, 124, 126, 127, 129, 130
steak sauce 116
stout beer 48
sweet pickle relish 108
sweet sherry 40, 45

T

tequila 50, 52, 54
teriyaki sauce 110, 114
thyme 107, 116
tomato 92
tomato paste 108

V

vegetable oil 74, 89
vodka 55

W

wasabi paste 103
whiskey 56, 58, 60, 61
white sugar 34, 39, 68, 79, 86, 89, 103, 112
white wine vinegar 70, 140
Worcestershire sauce 27, 28, 30, 36, 40, 56, 58, 78, 82, 90, 99, 108, 109, 124, 126, 130, 135, 136, 140

NOTES

NOTES

NOTES

NOTES

NOTES